JEHOVAH'S

CONFUCIANISM

TANISM

One God,
many gods

SIKHISM

SCIENTOLO

By Adam Francisco

HINDUISM   ISLAM

SHINTO

ORMONISM

BUDDHISM

NEW AGE

NISM   CONCORDIA PUBLISHING HOUSE · SAINT LOUIS

DAOISM

Written by Adam Francisco

Edited by Mark S. Sengele

This publication may be available in braille, in large print, or on cassette tape for the visually impaired. Please allow 8 to 12 weeks for delivery. Write to Lutheran Blind Mission, 7550 Watson Rd., St. Louis, MO 63119-4409; call toll-free 1-888-215-2455; or visit the Web site: www.blindmission.org.

Manufactured in the United States of America

Your comments and suggestions concerning the material are appreciated. Please write the Editor of Youth Materials, Concordia Publishing House, 3558 S. Jefferson Ave., St. Louis, MO 63118-3968.

2 3 4 5 6 7 8 9 10 11   22 21 20 19 18 17 16 15 14 13

Table of Contents

Introduction

Beloved, do not believe every spirit, but test the spirits to see whether they are from God, for many false prophets have gone out into the world. By this you know the Spirit of God: every spirit that confesses that Jesus Christ has come in the flesh is from God, and every spirit that does not confess Jesus is not from God. This is the spirit of the antichrist, which you heard was coming and now is in the world already. Little children, you are from God and have overcome them, for He who is in you is greater than he who is in the world. They are from the world; therefore they speak from the world, and the world listens to them. We are from God. Whoever knows God listens to us; whoever is not from God does not listen to us. By this we know the Spirit of truth and the spirit of error. 1 John 4:1–6

We live in an increasingly interconnected world. We are now able to communicate with people of different cultures with the click of a button. Information is available twenty-four hours a day and seven days a week through the Internet. Traveling overseas is also relatively easy and affordable these days. But you don't have to travel to a different country to experience a different culture. America is a country of considerable cultural and ethnic diversity. Nowhere are these differences more obvious than in the various religions scattered about America's cities and even its rural areas. People of those faiths now live next door to us, work with us, build houses of worship in our neighborhoods, and even find converts among our friends.

One God, many gods is a Bible study resource for this demographic trend. Christianity and fourteen other religious faiths are examined and compared, with a goal of identifying the central teachings of each and providing some tools for Christians who encounter people of other faiths in their daily lives. The subjects and the Bible studies in this book are appropriate for high-school-age young people through older adults.

Each of the fifteen studies follows a similar format. (The first is slightly different.) It generally begins with an opening question for discussion. An opening activity can be substituted for the discussion, but a discussion is preferable, for it helps generate an atmosphere of dialogue. Following this, the study then hones in on the essential history and teachings of a particular world religion. This is followed by a consideration of how a Christian might respond to the particular non-Christian religion with the Gospel.

Why Study Other Religions?

Religion is inherent in all cultures and all people. This study then is a study of people and their core beliefs. Undertaking such a study is beneficial for the following reasons:

- We may better understand people of other faiths, so that we do not fear or avoid them but are able to interact with them from a base knowledge. We will have "points of contact" from which conversations may arise.
- We may be able to demonstrate our sincere love for them as people and learn how to help them without offending them.

- We may grow in compassion for the 3.7 billion people who do not know the one, true God. They are people who need the Gospel, who do not know the benefit of God's grace in His Word and Sacraments.
- We may be better able to avoid their false religious views and hold more firmly to our Christian faith. It can be helpful to test the mettle of our convictions against the beliefs of others.
- We are not alone. We cannot avoid increased contact with other religions in the twenty-first century, but we can be prepared for such contact.
- We have a compelling need to share Jesus Christ with others. To a world with many gods, we can offer the blessing of faith in the one God who is the only Creator, Redeemer, and Sanctifier of all people. This is a truth that we cannot help but share.

Suggestions for Adapting and Using These Studies

It is not required that all fifteen studies in this book be taught or that they be taught in a particular order. While most groups will benefit from reviewing the basic teachings of Christianity in session 1, some may prefer to skip this study or use it as a conclusion. (You may desire even more background study in the Christian faith before or after tackling these studies. *Solid Truth: Bible Studies for Postmodern Teens* is a set of twelve topical studies based on the Apostles' Creed. It would be a logical choice for youth Bible classes.)

If you decide to use only some of the studies initially, consider these points as you make your choices:

- What religions are prominent in current events now?
- What religions are prominent in your community?
- What religions are prominent in the media?

Finally, while these studies will meet the needs of many groups, you may need to alter it in order to make it fit the needs and characteristics of your group.

Resources

It will be useful to have some additional resources available for further research as you prepare for these studies. Here is just a preliminary list:

Thomas Manteufel, *Churches in America* (CPH, 1994)

How to Respond Series (CPH, 1995), including

 Erwin J. Kolb, *Judaism*

 Ernest Hahn, *Muslims*

 Bruce G. Frederickson, *Satanism*

 Edgar P. Kaiser, *The Latter-day Saints*

 Herbert Kern, *Jehovah's Witnesses*

 Hubert F. Beck, *The Cults*

 Philip H. Lochhaas, *The New Age Movement*

George A. Mather and Larry A. Nichols, *Dictionary of Cults, Sects, Religions and the Occult* (Zondervan, 2006)

Josh McDowell and Don Stewart, *Handbook of Today's Religions* (Thomas Nelson, 1996)

Anthony J. Steinbronn, *Worldviews: A Christian Response to Religious Pluralism* (CPH, 2007)

Leaders are strongly encouraged to obtain the *Dictionary of Cults, Sects, Religions, and the Occult* and read the relevant entry as they prepare for the particular studies in this book.

1
Christianity

Lesson Focus

Christians live in a world that is growing increasingly diverse. Other faiths, which offer alternative and opposing beliefs to Christianity, seem to be flourishing. To defend the veracity of Christianity and even to engage non-Christian religions requires a firm grounding in our own faith.

Opening Discussion

Before class, write *sin* and *redemption* on a whiteboard or newsprint. Have the class discuss what the terms mean. After arriving at a definition, explain to the class that the people we come into contact with each week may come from different religions or have no religion at all. For many of them, the terms on the board—words that many of you found easy to explain—are concepts that carry no meaning. But these concepts are integral to the Christian faith. Before investigating other religions, it is important that we have a solid understanding of the Christian faith.

Pray the following,

Dear heavenly Father, help us grow in our knowledge and willingness to tell others how You, through the death and resurrection of Your Son, reconciled the world unto Yourself. We have friends, neighbors, and colleagues who do not know this. So for Your sake we ask that You empower us to reach out and engage those unbelievers with whom we come into contact. We ask this in the name of Jesus, who lives and reigns with

You and the Holy Spirit, one God, now and forever. Amen.

The Essence of Christianity

Begin by asking the students what the chief source of authority for the core of the Christian message is. After students have expressed themselves, explain to them that in order to understand the basic and essential teachings of the Christian faith, one must first and foremost turn to and understand the Scriptures. Assure them that this is not as daunting of a task as one might fear. We know from Scripture itself that ultimately the whole Bible testifies to the incarnation, life, death, and resurrection of Christ (Luke 24:25–27). And so the Scriptures must be viewed in light of these events. There is still quite an enormous amount of material in the biblical text, but theologians have combed through the biblical narrative over the centuries, and they have found a way to help organize our thinking about how God has revealed Himself in the Scriptures.

The fundamental key to interpreting Scripture, and thus to understanding the essence of the Christian faith, is the distinction between Law and Gospel. It is "a particularly brilliant light. It serves the purpose of rightly dividing God's Word [2 Timothy 2:15] and properly explaining and understanding the Scriptures" (SD V 1). Provide copies of Participant Page 1 and have a volunteer read the Solid Declaration of the Formula of Concord V 23–24.

Assign students to look up the passages found in this quote from the confessions that are listed on the Participant Page. Ask students to look for common themes or messages. Review their reflections with the whole group.

Genesis 3:15—The serpent's (Satan's) head will be bruised (NIV says "crushed") by the promised Savior. This is the first glimpse of God's plan of salvation, also called the "protoevangelium" or the first Gospel.

Genesis 22:18—All the nations of the earth will be blessed through Abraham's offspring.

Genesis 28:14—In Jacob's dream, God promises to bless all the families of the earth through Jacob's offspring.

Psalm 110:1—God promises to make David's enemies his "footstool."

Isaiah 40:10—The Lord comes in might; He will rule over His people and receive His just reward.

Isaiah 49:6—God will make the descendent of Jacob a "light for the nations" who brings His salvation to the ends of the earth.

Isaiah 53:5—Christ was "wounded for our transgressions," "crushed for our iniquities," and chastised to bring us peace, true peace with God and man that has come through His suffering.

Luke 2:32—The infant Christ is the light for the Gentiles and the glory for the chosen people of Israel.

Romans 10:4—Christ is the end of the Law; He brings righteousness to all believers.

Galatians 3:24—The Law was with us until we were justified by Christ.

2 Corinthians 3:7–9—The ministry of righteousness has won out over the ministry of death.

The goal is to get students to see that: (1) The two key doctrines of Scripture are the doctrine of the Law, that human beings are utterly sinful and continually commit sinful deeds, and the Gospel, that God promised to resolve the miserable situation Adam and Eve and all subsequent generations of human beings found themselves in after the fall. (2) God accomplished this ultimately by sending His Son to offer Himself as an all-atoning sacrifice for the sins of the world. This teaching of Law and Gospel or of sin and reconciliation is the consensus of all of Scripture (Acts 10:43). Grasping these two doctrines is essential for evaluating the claims of other religions.

Essentials for Sharing Christ

Begin this section by having a student read 2 Corinthians 5:11–21. Discuss what this passage means. In particular, ask students to explain what Paul probably meant in verse 11, when he said that "knowing the fear of the Lord, we persuade others." Also, discuss what it means to be an ambassador for Christ.

Emphasize that, in sharing our faith with non-Christians, the first and most important step is to share the message of the Law, that we are all sinners in need of a Savior, and the Gospel, that through Christ's death on the cross our sins and the sins of the world were paid for. Our relationship with God was restored during three days in Jerusalem, when Jesus was crucified but rose again from the dead. This is the message all people desperately need to hear.

Be sure to stress that this isn't just "pie-in-the-sky" religious opinion. This is a brute and accomplished fact. The reconciliation won for us by Christ on the cross is both a theological and a historical fact. So a Christian witness to the Gospel isn't just an exchange of ideas but a claim to fact. No other religion can claim to be factual in the way Christianity can. Give the students a moment to consider this and to ask any questions they might have; then close the session with prayer.

Closing

Conclude with this prayer:

Dear Jesus, You paid an incredible price for each one of us. You gave Your life so that we can spend eternity with You. Thank You for Your love and constant care. We know other people who need the salvation only You can offer. Send Your Holy Spirit into their hearts. Use us to tell them the story of how You took upon Yourself human flesh, lived among us, died at our hands, but rose victoriously three days later. Be with those who are in need. Give them healing of mind and body and the assurance of Your love. In Your most holy and blessed name we pray. Amen.

1
CHRISTIANITY

The Essence of Christianity

Using Law and Gospel

From the beginning of the world, these two proclamations have always been taught alongside each other in God's Church, with a proper distinction. The descendants of the well-respected patriarchs, and the patriarchs themselves, called to mind constantly how in the beginning a person had been created righteous and holy by God. They know that through the fraud of the serpent, Adam transgressed God's command, became a sinner, and corrupted and cast himself with all his descendants into death and eternal condemnation. They encouraged and comforted themselves again by the preaching about the woman's seed, who would bruise the serpent's head (**Genesis 3:15**); Abraham's seed, in whom "all the nations of the earth [will] be blessed" (**Genesis 22:18**); David's Son, who should "bring back the preserved of Israel" and be "a light for the nations" (**Isaiah 49:6**; see also **Psalm 110:1**; **Luke 2:32**), and who "was wounded for our transgressions; He was crushed for our iniquities . . . and with His stripes we are healed" (**Isaiah 53:5**).

Genesis 3:15

Genesis 22:18

Genesis 28:14

Psalm 110:1

Isaiah 40:10

Isaiah 49:6

Isaiah 53:5

Luke 2:32

Romans 10:4

Galatians 3:24

2 Corinthians 3:7–9

These two doctrines, we believe and confess, should always be diligently taught in God's Church forever, even to the end of the world. They must be taught with the proper distinction of which we have heard: (1) through the preaching of the Law and its threats in the ministry of the New Testament the hearts of impenitent people may be terrified, and (2) they may be brought to a knowledge of their sins and to repentance. This must not be done in such a way that they lose heart and despair in this process. " 'So then, the law was our guardian until Christ came, in order that we might be justified by faith' (**Galatians 3:24**); so the Law points and leads us not from Christ, but to Christ, who 'is the end of the law' (**Romans 10:4**)" (SD V 23–24).

Participant Page 1 *One God, many gods* © 2008 Concordia Publishing House. Scripture: ESV™. *Concordia: The Lutheran Confessions*, second edition, © 2006 Concordia Publishing House. All rights reserved. Reproduced by permission.

2
Judaism

Lesson Focus

All Christian religions have at their core Judaism, since it is within the context of Judaism that our Lord and Savior came to earth. Today's Jews bear little resemblance to the historic Jewish people of Christ's time.

Opening Discussion

Judaism has in the past been the second largest religion in America. (It may still be, although some have suggested that Islam is quickly moving into this place.) Chances are your students have a Jewish friend or acquaintance. Ask students to explain what they've observed about Judaism or, if no one knows a Jew personally, what they know about Judaism.

Understanding Judaism

Explain how, of all the other religions, Christianity finds its closest kinship with Judaism. We share with Judaism many beliefs, including the authenticity and divine authority of the Old Testament as well as hope in the Messiah and resurrection. But most Jews do not yet share our faith in Jesus as the fulfillment of the Old Testament prophecies for the Messiah and the source of salvation from our sin.

Distribute copies of Participant Page 2, found at the end of this lesson, and direct students to the section concerning the history and teachings of Judaism. Have the students read through the information provided and discuss the nature of contemporary Judaism. You may

also want students to consider questions they might like to ask an expert in Judaism.

Have students note that of the three major divisions of Judaism in America, only Orthodox Jews are still waiting for the coming of the promised Messiah. Also, a significant number of people would also identify themselves as having a Jewish heritage but are not necessarily practicing the ancient faith of the Jews.

Responding to Judaism

We share many common beliefs and practices with Judaism. Many elements of liturgical worship have their roots in the worship forms used in the synagogue. Most Jews will be familiar with Jesus, but they won't acknowledge Him as the Savior. Because of their belief that the Messiah has not yet come, we can witness to Jews by celebrating the hope we have in Jesus. While an active, dynamic faith that openly confesses Jesus is essential, ask the students what other ways a Christian can help clear up any obstacles a Jew might have with the Gospel.

Because Christians and Jews both hold the Old Testament to be authoritative, Christians can and ought to use its numerous messianic prophecies to get Jews to consider the claims of Christianity. Assign students one or more of the passages found on the Participant Page and summarize what they say concerning the Messiah. When students have completed their work, review their findings with the whole group.

Genesis 12:1–3, 7—God calls Abram as His own and promises that Abram's offspring will be a great nation and that through Abram's offspring all people will be blessed. God shows Abram the land that has been promised to His people; it is the present-day location of the nation of Israel.

Genesis 49:10—As Jacob blesses his sons, he prophesies that the rule shall not depart from Judah until the Promised One comes.

Deuteronomy 8:15–19—God is the one who has led the people through the wilderness and given them manna and water. God will confirm His covenant made many generations before.

Isaiah 7:14—A virgin will conceive and bear a Son who will be called Immanuel.

Micah 5:2—The One who will come to rule Israel will be born in Bethlehem. He will be of old, from ancient days.

Jeremiah 31:31–34—The day is coming when God will make a new covenant with His people. He will put His Law in their hearts, and He will forgive their sins and remember them no more.

Isaiah 61:1–2—The Spirit of God is upon His servant; He will bring Good News to the poor, bind the brokenhearted, proclaim liberty to the captives, and open the prisons of those bound in sin. He will proclaim God's favor on His people and comfort those who mourn.

Isaiah 52:13; 53:3–12—God's servant will act wisely. He will be lifted up and exalted. Chapter 53 recounts much of the language used to describe Christ's suffering, death, and resurrection. The chapter concludes with the words "He bore the sin of many, and makes intercession for the transgressors" (Isaiah 53:12).

Jonah 1:17–2:10—Jonah entered his watery grave (the belly of the fish) and three days later was brought out of this "entombment." Jonah's prayer while within the fish reflects much of the work of Christ on this earth.

After students have summarized the prophecies concerning Christ, ask, *What evidence is there that Jesus was in fact the promised Messiah?* (He fulfilled all of the prophecies spoken about Him in the Old Testament.) *How is it possible the Jews missed the message?* (Jesus didn't fit their expectation of a political Messiah who would remove the Roman oppression and restore the Jews to self-governance.)

Closing

Conclude with the following prayer:

Loving Father, through the Old Testament patriarchs and prophets, You revealed Your plan of salvation. Help us use our knowledge of that history to build relationships with those who are still looking for the Messiah. Through our words and actions, help us share our faith with them so that they might see the hope that can be found only in Jesus Christ. Through the power of Your Holy Spirit, may that be accomplished through us. Amen.

2
JUDAISM

Understanding Judaism

History and Teachings

Judaism traces its roots back to Abraham in 2000 BC. God's promise to Abraham (Genesis 12:1–3) and His covenant with him (Genesis 15:1–21) begin the relationship between God and the Jewish people. In addition to Abraham, the other Old Testament patriarchs such as Moses, Isaac, Jacob, and others are revered by Jews. King David is also honored, because under him Israel became a mighty world power.

In the nineteenth century, Judaism divided into three groups—orthodox, conservative, and reformed. Teachings vary widely among these groups, with Reformed Judaism allowing significant departures from the traditional Jewish beliefs expressed in this summary.

There are around six million Jews living in America. A majority of these are practicing Jews. Almost every major city has at least one Jewish synagogue. Jewish people are very visible in our culture. In the entertainment industry, individuals such as Steven Spielberg and Barbara Streisand are practicing Jews. Jews can be found among the leaders in government, science, and business too.

In Judaism, God is conceived of as personal, all-powerful, eternal, and compassionate. His history with His people and His basic teachings are found in the Torah, the first five books of the Old Testament. Judaism also accepts as true the entire Old Testament and the Talmud, a multi-volume record of the teachings of the ancient rabbis.

Judaism stresses obedience to the Law (the Ten Commandments). While Jews acknowledge the necessity of God's mercy since no one can perfectly keep the Law, they do not acknowledge the substitutionary sacrifice of Jesus. Atonement for sin is made through works of righteousness, prayer, and repentance. Many Jews believe in a physical resurrection. Judaism does not accept Jesus Christ as the promised Messiah. To Jews, He is either a false prophet or a martyred teacher. Orthodox Jews believe the true Messiah is still to come. The Messiah's arrival will mean the restoration of the Jewish nation and His physical rule on the earth.

Responding to Judaism

What does each of these passages tell us about the promised Messiah?

Genesis 12:1–3, 7

Genesis 49:10

Deuteronomy 8:15–19

Isaiah 7:14

Micah 5:2

Jeremiah 31:31–34

Isaiah 61:1–2

Isaiah 52:13; 53:3–12

Jonah 1:17–2:10

3

Islam

Lesson Focus

Considered by many to be the fastest growing religious body worldwide, much is misunderstood about the true teachings of Islam. This lesson focuses on the need to clearly understand the teachings of Islam in order to share the Gospel with those who are lost without Christ.

Opening Discussion

Islam is obviously a hot topic in our world today. Students will likely have opinions to share concerning this religious group. To keep the opening discussion from devolving into a vitriolic rant about Islamic terrorism, begin by asking: *Many people assert that Christianity and Islam are two very similar religions that worship the same God. What do you think?* (While the world may believe this statement to be true, most Christian young people should recognize the fallacy in this statement.)

Understanding Islam

Distribute copies of Participant Page 3, which covers the history and teachings of Islam. Be prepared to answer additional questions concerning the teachings of Islam. (Since it is such a frequent topic in our society, you will want to do some additional reading on Islam. *How to Respond: Muslims* [12-6010] is a great place to start.)

Once you have reviewed the basic history and teachings, ask these two questions: *Does Islam share the same God as Christianity?* (While individual Muslims have some concept that there is one, true God, the god that the Qur'an informs them of is not the God of Christianity. The Qur'an rejects that Allah is three persons in the one divine essence.) *Doesn't Islam revere Jesus and therefore share some common beliefs alongside Christianity?* (Actually the Qur'an envisions a different Jesus. The Qur'an does teach that Jesus was born of the Virgin Mary. It also teaches that Jesus performed many miracles. But the Qur'an rejects that Jesus was the Son of God, that He died on the cross, and that He rose from the dead. Jesus is only a human messenger or prophet of God in Islam. This is a different Jesus than the Jesus of history, testified to and revealed to us in the Scriptures.)

Responding to Islam

It is important to stress to students that Christians have nothing to fear from Muslims. While the more radical ideas of Islam (especially the instructions to kill non-Muslims in Qur'an 9:5 and 29) may certainly be a cause for alarm, most Muslims (not all) in America are passive and want nothing more than to make ends meet and provide for their families. As Christians, we may very well work alongside these Muslim people and use the relationships that develop as a means to share the Gospel with them.

What about Muslims who assert the more radical aspects of Islam publicly? Have students read and discuss Luke 6:27–36. This fairly well-known section of Scripture contains Jesus' words concerning love for our enemies. This is not a call to pacifism but a call to courage. Encourage students to become bold witnesses to the Gospel both in word and deed to their Muslim neighbors and friends.

Ask the students, *Other than being kind and merciful, what is the best way to witness to a Muslim?* (There are numerous approaches, and they all have their strengths.) Christian missionaries who work in the Muslim community say that one of the best ways to witness to someone of the Muslim faith is to get them to read one of the Gospels. The Qur'an speaks positively of the Gospel that Jesus brought, but most Muslims have never had a chance or the desire to read Matthew, Mark, Luke, or John. It is in reading the Word of God that the Holy Spirit will most assuredly work.

If you have additional time, you may want to share information about People of the Book Lutheran Outreach (POBLO). This LCMS World Missions outreach to Arabic-speaking individuals has a number of sites throughout the country. Visit www.lcms.org for more information.

Closing

Conclude the study with prayer:

Heavenly Father, we thank You that Jesus was not only Your prophet, but also Your Son and our Savior. We praise You for His death, because it gives us life. We praise You for His life, because it gives us a future and a hope. Help us trust what You have revealed to us about Yourself, and help us understand the Islamic faith, that we may clearly witness to our faith to fellow Christians, Muslims, and people of no faith at all. Grant this to us, Father, because of Your Son, in whose name we pray. Amen.

3 ISLAM

Understanding Islam

History and Teachings

Muslim tradition claims that Allah ("god" in Arabic) began to reveal himself to a pious Arab named Muhammad (AD 570–632) beginning in the year 610. Eventually Muhammad began to preach these messages to his fellow countrymen in the city of Mecca. The message was not received well at first, but eventually Muhammad was able to gain a significant following when he moved from Mecca to Medina in 622.

In Medina, Muhammad enjoyed political and military control. And it was from here that he and the Muslims began their program for the expansion of Islam. Within a decade, most of the Arabian Peninsula was under the control of Islam. One hundred years after Muhammad's death in 632, an Islamic empire stretched from Spain and Morocco in the west to the western border of India in the east. Today, Islamic culture, but not total Islamic political control, stretches from as far east as Indonesia to Turkey and Morocco. It has made inroads into Europe, too, and is on the rise as a significant religious force in America.

What does Islam teach? The primary creed of Islam (*shahada*) is "There is no god but Allah, and Muhammad is his messenger." The primary source of authority in Islam is the Qur'an. Islam is a monotheistic religion. It teaches that there is only one god. Allah is unlike the one true God of Christianity though. The god of Islam is not a father; he does not have a son. In fact, the Qur'an teaches that to suggest as much is a heresy worthy of damnation.

The chief goal of a Muslim is to submit to Allah. (In fact, the term *Islam* means "submission to Allah," and a Muslim is one who is in a state of submission to Islam.) How does a Muslim do this? It is primarily by following the Five Pillars: (1) the *shahada* (see above); (2) prayer five times a day (*salah*); (3) charity to the tune of 2.5 percent of one's wealth (*zakah*); (4) fasting during the month of Ramadan (*Sawm*), the ninth month of the Muslim calendar when Muslims commemorate the beginning of the revelations given to Muhammad; and (5) making a pilgrimage to Mecca at least once in your life (*Hajj*), if you are physically and financially able to.

In addition to these individual requirements, Islam also provides political and legal instructions. Islam is not a private religious belief. Rather, it is an all-encompassing ideology, and it is a universal ideology. Thus the Qur'an enjoins Muslims to cause Islam to prevail over all other religions. Muslims are to devote their lives to the struggle (*jihad*) for what the Qur'an calls the "cause of Allah." This primarily takes the form of political, juridical, and physical or militaristic struggle. The claims that jihad is really a personal struggle with sin are misguided. The political, legal, and violent nature of jihad has always had pride of place in Islamic thought.

Islam is manifesting itself in a variety of ways today. There are some Muslims who have altered the traditional teachings of Islam so that it is amenable to liberal Western values. And there are some who take Islam to the opposite extreme. It is important to remember that although various Muslim communities interpret their religion differently, Islam as it is taught in the Qur'an is aggressive and universal in its agenda.

4

Hinduism

Lesson Focus

While most American youth may be unfamiliar with the specific teachings of Hinduism, they are likely familiar with yoga, a practice that flows from and is part of Hinduism. In this lesson, we go beyond this simple understanding to take a deeper look at Hinduism and how we as Christians can respond to those who need true spiritual enlightenment.

Opening Discussion

Ask the class if they know any Hindus or if they know anything about Hinduism. Ask: *What is reincarnation? Have you ever heard of or even practiced yoga?* (Allow students to share what they know about reincarnation and yoga. Reincarnation teaches that at death you return to earth in a different form, based on how you have lived your life. Yoga combines a series of stretches and physical positions with deep breathing, focused concentration, and meditation.) Note that while yoga ultimately originates in Hinduism, it is important not to insinuate that someone who has practiced yoga is necessarily practicing Hinduism. One should, however, be very cautious not to assume some of the teachings associated with yoga.

Understanding Hinduism

Distribute copies of Participant Page 4, which covers the history and teachings of Hinduism. Have the students discuss what they find particularly peculiar about Hindu teachings.

Allow students to work in pairs or small groups to study the list of essential Hindu teaching, and then read the suggested Scripture verses. What do these verses tell us about the differences between Hinduism and Christianity?

Hinduism teaches that the entirety of creation is divine (*Brahman*). Psalm 33:6, 9 (Christianity teaches that God is separate from creation.)

Hinduism teaches that there are multiple deities (although they are all part of the one unified whole). Deuteronomy 6:4; John 15:26 (Christianity teaches that there is one God—although there are three persons in the one divine essence.)

Because it associates anything in creation with the divinity, Hinduism sees Jesus as just one god among a multitude of others. 1 Corinthians 8:4–6 (Christianity teaches that Jesus is true God, the second person of the Trinity, one with God the Father and God the Holy Spirit.)

Hinduism teaches that humans can through their own merits obtain salvation or release from the cycle of reincarnation. Romans 3:22–24; 1 Peter 2:24 (Christianity teaches that all have sinned and fall short of the glory of God, but Christ took our sins upon Himself for our forgiveness and salvation.)

Hinduism teaches that there are numerous deities, represented by a multitude of idols, worthy of worship and devotion. Exodus 20:3–5; Jeremiah 10:5. (God forbids us to worship idols; these images do us no good.)

Hinduism teaches that one has numerous lives. Hebrews 9:27–28 (Christianity teaches that we only die once.)

These differences are vital for understanding how Christianity relates to Hinduism. If time permits, you might ask the class if they see any theological common ground between Christianity and Hinduism. Point out that while there may be some common ethical concerns, there are no theological ones. These vast differences are important to our understanding of how to witness to a Hindu believer.

Responding to Hinduism

Explain to the class that in addition to many of its other teachings, the Hindu concept of salvation is antithetical to Christianity's. Hinduism teaches that the road to salvation is circular. The human soul is repeatedly reborn as determined by its previous life and the law of karma until it is liberated from the cycle of reincarnation. At this point, Hinduism teaches, it becomes one with Brahman. To those trapped in such a fictitious and hopeless cycle, the one true God, the Father, offers the merits of His own Son, Jesus Christ, a single life of faith and service, and the joy of a guaranteed eternity with Him when we die.

Discuss with the class how one might bear witness to the need for Christ's merits for personal salvation. It is important to note that unless one recognizes that they are in fact by nature sinful and unclean, they will not see a need for a Savior. *What might this tell us about our approach to Hindus?* (In addition to sharing the Gospel, it is vital to explain how all have sinned and fallen short of the glory of God, for without the Law the Gospel is irrelevant.)

Closing

Conclude with the following prayer:

Dear heavenly Father, forgive our efforts to earn Your approval and our complete failure to do so. Move us by Your Holy Spirit to share the need for forgiveness with others. In Jesus' name we pray. Amen.

4
HINDUISM

Understanding Hinduism

History and Teachings

The origins of Hinduism are uncertain, but we do know that it is an ancient religion with roots in India. It has no single founder but numerous sacred texts. The earliest are known as the *Vedas*, which date back to at least 1000 BC. Perhaps the most famous Hindu in recent history was Mahatma Gandhi (1869–1948). Using Hindu principles of nonviolence, he led India in a mass passive protest of British rule, which ultimately ended in the British withdrawal from the subcontinent.

Hinduism is also found in America in many different forms. Both the transcendental meditation and Hare Krishna movements are expressions of Hinduism. Meditation and yoga have become common forms of stress release in our society, with classes offered at numerous colleges and fitness centers. Many celebrities, such as George Harrison of the Beatles, have been attracted to Hinduism.

Hinduism is often described as a polytheistic religion. Indeed, it is said that there are over 330 million gods in Hinduism. In reality, Hinduism teaches what scholars call pantheistic monism, a religious philosophy that teaches that everything shares in the entire divinity of the universe (*Brahman*). The souls of human beings share in this divinity. They thus survive after the death of the body and transmigrate until they are reincarnated in a different (human, animal, or plant) body. The cycle of soul transmigration and reincarnation is determined by a force called *karma* (deeds in one's present life determine one's status in the next); this cycle or process is called *samsara*. The overall goal of a Hindu is to be released from this cycle (*moksha*) and be reunited with the universal world soul (*atman*).

There are other teachings integral to Hinduism. Traditional Hinduism teaches that one is incarnated in a particular and fixed level or *caste* of society. *Gurus* are often sought out for guidance in one's attempt at realizing the divinity within and connection to the one divinity— *Brahman*. Various spiritual disciplines, purification rites, pilgrimages to sacred places, religious study, temple worship, observation of holy days, and rites of passage at significant times of life all aid in this self- and god-realization. Because of its monistic belief, Hinduism typically teaches that there is no one religion that leads to salvation. Instead, they all can, so long as they facilitate one's quest for personal enlightenment and realization.

What is the Christian's response to each of these Hindu teachings?

Hinduism teaches that the entirety of creation is divine (*Brahman*). **Psalm 33:6, 9**

Hinduism teaches that there are multiple deities (although they are all part of the one unified whole). **Deuteronomy 6:4; John 15:26**

Because it associates anything in creation with the divinity, Hinduism sees Jesus as just one god among a multitude of others. **1 Corinthians 8:4–6**

Hinduism teaches that humans can through their own merits obtain salvation or release from the cycle of reincarnation. **Romans 3:22–24; 1 Peter 2:24**

Hinduism teaches that there are numerous deities, represented by a multitude of idols, worthy of worship and devotion. **Exodus 20:3–5; Jeremiah 10:5**

Hinduism teaches that one has numerous lives. **Hebrews 9:27–28**

5

Buddhism

Lesson Focus

Buddhism shares many beliefs with its root religion Hinduism, particularly the belief in reincarnation. These ardent followers of Buddha desperately need to hear the truth of the Gospel.

Opening Discussion

Begin the class by asking students, *What comes to mind when you think of Buddhism and Buddhists?* (One of the most striking aspects of Buddhism is its seeming humility. Buddhists are typically very kind and gentle. Students may also recall the robes associated with Buddhist clerics or the many round-bellied figures of Buddha available.) Point out to the class that while the humbleness of Buddhism is genuine, it is one of many requirements for salvation from the cycle of reincarnation.

Understanding Buddhism

Distribute copies of Participant Page 5 and have students read through the history and teachings of Buddhism. After the students have had time to read through this information, discuss the Four Noble Truths, affirming them when possible but criticizing their shortcomings.

1. Suffering is universal. Job 14:1; Ecclesiastes 2:23 (This is basically true. Because of sin the world is full of all kinds of suffering.)

2. Suffering is caused by desire. Romans 7:21–25 (This is partly true. Our attachment to the world does cause much of our suffering,

but in Buddhism desire results in suffering because our desire is for a world that is ultimately not what it appears to be. According to Buddhist teachings, the world is an illusion. According to Scripture, the real cause of our suffering is the constant battle between our sinful human flesh and our desire to fulfill the Law. Only Christ can rescue us from this situation.)

3. To eliminate suffering is to eliminate desire. 1 John 5:4–5 (If suffering was caused only by our selfish desires, then the solution would be to get rid of selfish desires as this "truth" proposes. However, point out that if drowning people could save themselves, they would not be drowning. In our sinful state where suffering is unavoidable, we are drowning in an ocean of sin. We need a rescuer. We can only overcome suffering through faith in God's Son.)

4. A path must be followed in order to achieve the Buddhist ideals. Ephesians 2:1; 2 Corinthians 5:17 (With reference to the Eightfold Path, draw attention to the inherent works-righteousness orientation of this so-called truth. Make the point that ultimately Buddhism relies on what human beings do. Our problem, however, is not just our impure thoughts or failure at achieving enlightenment. We are drowning, totally

incapable of helping ourselves. Our sin has made us dead; it is only through Christ that we have life.)

Responding to Buddhism

Have students look at each of the steps of the Eightfold Path and the suggested Scripture verse. How does the verse address that stage of the path?

1. Right views—accepting the truth of the Four Noble Truths and legitimacy of the Eightfold Path. Proverbs 1:7 (All understanding begins with knowing the true God.)

2. Right thought—denying the pleasure of the world, causing no harm, and harboring no ill will toward anybody. Matthew 6:33 (Our purpose is to seek God.)

3. Right speech—avoiding idle talk, lying, and slander. Ephesians 4:29 (Use words that build one another up.)

4. Right conduct—avoiding killing a living creature, being content with what you have, and being sexually pure. Exodus 20:13–15 (You shall not murder, commit adultery, or steal.)

5. Right vocation—avoiding a vocation that causes harm to any other sentient creature. Galatians 5:14 (Love your neighbor as yourself.)

6. Right effort—ridding oneself of negative and harmful qualities and growing in positive and helpful ones. Colossians 3:12–14 (Put on Christlike virtues.)

7. Right alertness or mind control—being alert, observant, thoughtful, and contemplative. Romans 12:1–2 (Renew your mind through God's Word.)

8. Right meditation—having abandoned all sensuous desires and bad qualities, one must then advance through various levels of meditation. 1 Thessalonians 5:16–18 (Be joyful, pray, and give thanks in Christ.)

Buddhists believe that one must follow these steps to achieve enlightenment. Have someone read Romans 6:23; then ask the class, *What is the inherent problem with this belief?* (The Eightfold Path cannot take us to God, because we need more than to be enlightened. What human beings really need is for someone to save us from drowning in our own sin. We cannot save ourselves. Only Christ, who is fully man and fully God, has the power to save us.)

Continue the class discussion by asking the students, *What do you think people find attractive about the Buddhist faith?* (Answers will of course vary. But point out that many people are drawn to Buddhism for its emphasis on mystical experience and enlightenment.) While Christianity is neither mystical nor does it teach enlightenment the way Buddhism does, Christianity does teach that God, in the person of the Holy Spirit, enlightens us with His gifts. *How has the Holy Spirit enlightened us?* (Discuss the importance and wonderful gifts received by Christians when they receive forgiveness and newness of life in their Baptism, when they hear the Word of God preached, and when they receive the body and blood of Christ in the Lord's Supper.)

Closing

Conclude with the following prayer:

Heavenly Father, we thank You that You have had mercy on us and saved us through the work of Your Son, Jesus Christ. Grant that we may by the power of the Holy Spirit bear witness to this truth at every opportunity. In Your name we pray. Amen.

5
BUDDHISM

Understanding Buddhism

History and Teachings

Buddhism emerged sometime around 500 BC. A wealthy prince named Siddhartha Gautama (563–483 BC) found some of the teachings of Hinduism inadequate, although he retained belief in reincarnation. His problem was with the insufficiency of Hinduism in explaining the suffering and pain he observed in the world. Through religious contemplation, Gautama discovered what he believed was the truth of life. He thus became known as "the enlightened one" or *Buddha*, and taught others his discoveries. Buddhism attracted many followers, and a variety of sects developed in different countries and cultures. Today, followers number over three hundred million worldwide. There are between two and five million in America.

Buddhism is best described as more a philosophy than a religion. Some have even called it atheistic, although some forms of Buddhism revere Buddha as a deity and speak of salvation through faith in him. Buddhism is a journey to an enlightened state of being. It is only by achieving this enlightened state of being that one can escape the endless cycle of reincarnation and achieve nirvana, where all of one's individuality is lost as the soul becomes extinguished. This is all achievable by accepting the Four Noble Truths and following the Eightfold Path.

The Four Noble Truths

1. Suffering is universal.
   Job 14:1; Ecclesiastes 2:23
2. Suffering is caused by desire.
   Romans 7:21–25
3. To eliminate suffering is to eliminate desire. **1 John 5:4–5**
4. A path must be followed in order to achieve this.
   Ephesians 2:1; 2 Corinthians 5:17

Responding to Buddhism

The Eightfold Path

1. Right views—accepting the truth of the Four Noble Truths and legitimacy of the Eightfold Path. **Proverbs 1:7**
2. Right thought—denying the pleasure of the world, causing no harm, and harboring no ill will toward anybody. **Matthew 6:33**
3. Right speech—avoiding idle talk, lying, and slander. **Ephesians 4:29**
4. Right conduct—avoiding killing a living creature, being content with what you have, and being sexually pure. **Exodus 20:13–15**
5. Right vocation—avoiding a vocation that causes harm to any other sentient creature. **Galatians 5:14**
6. Right effort—ridding oneself of negative and harmful qualities and growing in positive and helpful ones. **Colossians 3:12–14**
7. Right alertness or mind control—being alert, observant, thoughtful, and contemplative. **Romans 12:1–2**
8. Right meditation—having abandoned all sensuous desires and bad qualities, one must then advance through various levels of meditation. **1 Thessalonians 5:16–18**

6

Sikhism

Lesson Focus

This lesson focuses on a religious group that is often misidentified. Through this study, we will explore the basic teachings of Sikhism and learn how to best approach these individuals with the Gospel of Jesus Christ.

Opening Discussion

Open the class with the following question: *When you see someone wearing a turban, what religion do you think they belong to? Why?* (Most will probably identify those who wear turbans as Muslims.) After the terrorist attacks on New York and Washington DC on September 11, 2001, the property of many Sikhs in America was vandalized because they were mistaken for Muslims. More often than not, those who wear turbans in American society are Sikhs.

After explaining that Sikhism will be the topic of the sessions, begin class with the following prayer:

> *We thank You, our heavenly Father, for bringing us together to learn about the people for whom You died. We ask that You grant us a passion for those who have not heard the Gospel and bless us with understanding and insight into how we might share our faith with them. In Your name. Amen.*

Understanding Sikhism

Distribute copies of Participant Page 6, found at the end of the study. Direct students to the history and teachings of Sikhism. After students have had a chance to read it, ask them what Sikh teachings share in common with Islam and Hinduism. *In terms of how one is saved, is Sikhism more like Islam or Hinduism?* (Like Islam, it believes in one transcendent God, but like Hinduism, it teaches that souls are reincarnated until they find their way out of the cycle.)

Responding to Sikhism

Explain to the class that in addition to many of its other teachings, the Sikh conception of salvation, like that of Hinduism, is antithetical to Christianity's. Sikhism teaches that the road to salvation is circular. The soul is repeatedly reborn until it is liberated from the cycle of reincarnation through meditation. At this point, Sikhism teaches, the soul becomes one with God. To those trapped in such a fictitious and hopeless cycle, the one true God, the Father, offers the merits of His own Son, Jesus Christ, a single life of faith and service, and the joy of a guaranteed eternity with Him when we die.

Discuss with the class how one might bear witness to the need for Christ's merits for personal salvation. It is important to note that unless people recognize that they are in fact by nature sinful and unclean, they will not see a need for a Savior. Assign pairs of students to read one of the selected Scripture verses listed on the Participant Page and summarize what the verse says. Have each pair report on their findings.

Ephesians 2:1—We were dead in our sin.

1 Corinthians 2:14—Without God's Spirit we cannot truly understand spiritual things. We must have God's Spirit to discern what they mean.

Romans 8:7–8—The sinful human mind is hostile toward God because it cannot keep God's Law. Sinners cannot please God.

Romans 3:21–24—There is a righteousness apart from the Law through the work of Jesus Christ. All have sinned and are opposed to God. We receive the free gift of justification through faith in Christ.

2 Corinthians 5:21—God the Father made His own Son to be sin on our behalf.

Romans 6:6—We have been crucified to sin in Christ so that we may no longer be slaves to sin.

What might these verses tell us about our approach to Sikhs? (In addition to sharing the Gospel, it is vital to explain how all have sinned and fallen short of the glory of God, for without the Law, the Gospel is irrelevant.)

Closing

Conclude the study with the following prayer:

Dear heavenly Father, forgive our efforts to earn Your approval and our complete failure to do so. Also forgive our prejudices against others, and move us to reach out to others of different cultures and religions with the message of salvation from sin through Your Son's atoning death and glorious resurrection. In Jesus' name we pray. Amen.

6
SIKHISM

Understanding Sikhism

History and Teachings

The founder of Sikhism was a religious teacher named Guru Nanak (1469–1539). He lived in what is now called Pakistan when it was populated by Hindus and Muslims, who were constantly antagonizing each other. Sikh tradition recounts how Nanak had a vision that he was to preach and teach a new religion. Shortly thereafter, when he was bathing in a stream, he disappeared and was sent into seclusion, only to return three days later to proclaim the principle teaching of Sikhism: There is no Hindu; there is no Muslim.

Guru Nanak was the first prophetic teacher of Sikhism. After his death, he was succeeded by one guru after another, all of which acted as prophets of Sikhism. At the time of the tenth guru, Gobind Rai (1675–1708), two developments occurred within the new religion. First, it was declared that the line of the gurus had come to an end. Second, the writings and hymns of the previous gurus were collected in a text called the *Siri Guru Granth Sahib*. The *Guru Granth* is the Sikh's primary source of religious authority.

Sikhism is a compilation of Hindu and Muslim beliefs. It teaches that there is one God, who created all things. But it also teaches that the created souls are forever caught up in the cycle of reincarnation (*samsara*) until they are able to escape it through the discipline of meditation. Sikhs gather to pray at temples called *gurdwaras*. Traditional Sikhs keep their hair long, although it is typically kept under a turban. They may also wear short pants, a metal bracelet, and a dagger (to remind them of the persecution they suffered under Muslims in the Punjab region of Pakistan).

Responding to Sikhism

Ephesians 2:1

1 Corinthians 2:14

Romans 8:7–8

Romans 3:21–24

2 Corinthians 5:21

Romans 6:6

7

Shinto

Lesson Focus

Shinto, the native religion of Japan, has many followers today. Their beliefs are filled with multiple gods and rituals steeped in tradition. Shinto adherents desperately need to hear the truth found in God's Word.

Opening Discussion

Begin class by reading Romans 1:18–23. Ask the students to discuss how this passage might explain the development of many (if not all) of the world's religions. The point is to get the students to see (1) that all people by nature know that a God exists; (2) rather than seeking out His clear revelation in the prophets, apostles, and Christ, they instead created idolatrous religions to account for this innate knowledge of God; and (3) some go so far as to attribute divinity to mere created things. Ask the class to consider this passage throughout their study of the Shinto religion.

Understanding Shinto

Distribute copies of Participant Page 6, found at the end of the study. Have students review the history and teachings of Shinto. Ask, *How might you characterize Shinto? How would you compare Christianity's view of God and creation with that of Shinto?* (Shinto is essentially nature worship, as gods [*kami*] are associated with various created elements and objects. Moreover, Shinto teaches that the gods can be appeased to manipulate nature for one's benefit.

Christianity teaches that God is differentiated from creation. Worship is directed at the Creator and not the creation.)

To illustrate this point, have the class contrast each Shinto teaching listed on the Participant Page with its respective Bible verse. Review with the whole class.

By worshiping and praying to your dead ancestors, you can receive direction and protection in life. Compare with Luke 12:22, 31 and Romans 1:25. (Don't be anxious about anything, but make your requests known to God. Those who worship the creation rather than the Creator have exchanged the truth for a lie.)

Sky-Father (*Iza Nagi*) and Earth-Mother (*Iza Nami*) gave birth to the earth, and that is how the world was created. Compare with Isaiah 40:28b. (The Lord is the "Creator of the ends of the earth.")

There is not one God but many spirits or gods worthy of worship. The spirits can be found in trees, rivers, mountains, and rocks. Compare with Deuteronomy 4:35. ("The Lord is God; there is no other besides Him.")

Rituals and offerings must be observed to prevent bad things. Compare with 1 John 4:18. ("Perfect love casts out fear.")

Various religions—even those with mutually exclusive teachings—can be fused together into one's own personal religion. Compare with Deuteronomy 5:7 and Isaiah 40:18. ("You shall have no other gods before Me." "To whom then will you liken God, or what likeness compare with Him?")

There is no real founder, no written scripture, and no static religious doctrine. Compare with 2 Timothy 3:16–17. (Scripture has been given for a purpose, so that we are equipped for all our needs.)

Human beings do not rule over the earth but are members of a community with other beings including animals, plants, minerals, and natural phenomena such as sky, water, mountain, and earth. Compare with Genesis 1:28–30. (God created mankind separately and has given them rule over all of creation.)

Everything from trees to buildings has a spirit. Compare with Genesis 1:26–27. (Humans were created in the image of God, having a spirit. The rest of creation does not.)

Responding to Shinto

Have the class reread Romans 1:18–23. *What insight might this provide in understanding the basic motifs of Shinto?* (Sinful humanity turned away from the truth and has created a religion based on a lie.)

Have the class read John 1:1–18. *How does the theology of John's prologue help in addressing the Shinto religion?* (Stress the unity of the pre-incarnate Word [Jesus] with God the Father; the triune God's eternal existence; the created and thus temporal existence of nature; the distinct difference between God and creation; and the unique revelation of God in Christ, who alone makes God known. It is only through the eternal Word of God that anyone can find temporal and eternal peace with God.)

Closing

Conclude by having someone read John 14:6–7, and then pray the following:

Father, we thank You for Your incredible grace. We know that we cannot earn Your favor by doing good works, whether it be through tradition, love of nature, cleanliness, or the observation of festivals and rituals. We know You love us. You loved us so much that You gave Your Son for us. And You planned it all before the creation of the world. Thank You for all You give us, and thank You for Your mercy. In Jesus' name we pray. Amen.

7
SHINTO

Understanding Shinto

History and Teachings

Shinto is the native religion of Japan. Although its historical origins are unclear, it is one of the oldest religions in the world. It has no real founder, no written scriptures, no body of religious law, and only a very loosely organized priesthood. Shinto is open to syncretism, that is, people may practice it alongside a second or even third religion. Most Japanese practice Shinto and Buddhism, although some have integrated ideas from Confucianism as well. In North America, there is a large and growing number of Japanese immigrants. Many of them will experiment with other religions (even Christianity) while maintaining Shinto beliefs.

Shinto is primarily a form of nature worship. Mountains, rivers, heavenly bodies, and other things are worshiped and personified. Scholars of religion call this *animism*. Shinto animism is based on the idea that the spirit (*anima*) is the seat of life. Everything has a spirit (*kami*) and will act according to its spirit. Human beings are not supreme rulers of the world but members of the community with other beings—animals, plants, minerals, and the like. Rules, rituals, and worship help to maximize agricultural harvests and bring blessings to social units or territories while preventing destruction and bad fortune.

If you were to ask someone who practices Shinto what their major teachings are, they would probably describe what are called the four affirmations:

- Affirmation of the tradition and the family.
- Affirmation of the love of nature.
- Affirmation of physical cleanliness.
- Affirmation of festivals honoring the spirits (matsuri).

The Shinto religion is expressed in all parts of life, such as architecture (Shinto shrines are made of wood and typically have flowing water nearby), art forms (like *origami*), and family life (for example, ancestor worship). Prayers and sacrifices to ancestors can be offered at family altars where ancestors are visibly present in tablets. For important decisions and important occasions of one's life, ancestors are consulted, that is, their graves are visited for reflection and meditation.

Compare these Shinto teachings with the words from Scripture.

By worshiping and praying to your dead ancestors, you can receive direction and protection in life. Compare with **Luke 12:22, 31** and **Romans 1:25**.

Sky-Father (*Iza Nagi*) and Earth-Mother (*Iza Nami*) gave birth to the earth, and that is how the world was created. Compare with **Isaiah 40:28b**.

There is not one God but many spirits or gods worthy of worship. The spirits can be found in trees, rivers, mountains, and rocks. Compare with **Deuteronomy 4:35**.

Rituals and offerings must be observed to prevent bad things. Compare with **1 John 4:18**.

Various religions—even those with mutually exclusive teachings—can be fused together into one's own personal religion. Compare with **Deuteronomy 5:7** and **Isaiah 40:18**.

There is no real founder, no written scripture, and no static religious doctrine. Compare with **2 Timothy 3:16–17**.

Human beings do not rule over the earth, but are members of a community with other beings including animals, plants, minerals, and natural phenomena such as sky, water, mountain, and earth. Compare with **Genesis 1:28–30**.

Everything from trees to buildings has a spirit. Compare with **Genesis 1:26–27**.

Responding to Shinto

Romans 1:18–23

John 1:1–18

John 14:6–7

8

Confucianism and Daoism

Lesson Focus

While students may readily identify yin and yang, they probably have no idea of their connection to the traditional religions of China. Through this study, students will examine the teachings of Confucianism and Daoism and how we as Christians can respond.

Opening Discussion

Begin the class by asking. *Do you know who Confucius was?* (He was a Chinese thinker and philosopher who lived some five hundred years before the time of Christ.) Then ask students to describe (and perhaps even to draw) the symbol for yin and yang. What does this symbol represent? (Two opposite yet complementary philosophies, such as Confucianism and Daoism.)

After explaining that both Confucianism and Daoism—even though they may seem strange to us—are religious philosophies held by millions of people, open with the following prayer:

> *Dear heavenly Father, we thank You for Your boundless mercy! You graciously looked upon us poor miserable sinners and sent Your Son to die for us, that we might live with You for all eternity. What great joy this brings to us. We ask that this joy would be evident in our lives and in our relationships, and*

> *that the Holy Spirit would empower us to share this joy with others. We know that the only way to You is through Him who lives and reigns with You and the Holy Spirit, one God, now and forever. Amen.*

Understanding Confucianism and Daoism

Distribute copies of Participant Page 8, which summarizes the history and teachings of Confucianism and Daoism. After reading through and explaining the sheet (with the help of additional texts if needed), ask the class what they think about Confucianism or Daoism.

At face value, Confucianism looks more like an innocuous familial and political ethic than a religion. Practically speaking, it generally is. However, its underlying convictions are deeply religious. It presumes there is a hidden and impersonal force guiding the universe forward in time and that human beings collectively are quite capable of conforming to the *Dao*, or way, upon which it is moving.

Daoism's religious or mystical character is a little more obvious. But we often fail to see its pervasiveness. Ask the class if they have ever witnessed a parade on the occasion of the Chinese New Year (toward the end of winter) when a very long paper dragon proceeds through the streets. Most will have at least seen pictures or media clips of this. Explain how the dragon represents the coming of yang energy as the days get longer and warmer as the season moves on toward summer. Six months later, at midsummer, the Chinese celebrate the coming of yin energy with the famous lion dances. The days shorten and the temperatures grow colder. Daoism (and even Confucianism) teaches that, by observing this and other rituals, one can achieve a proper balance between these two energies. This enables one to conform to the *Dao*.

Have the class then discuss the follow question: *From the brief study, can you surmise what Confucianism and Daoism teach about the nature of human beings?* (Be sure to emphasize that both see humans as inherently good and capable of doing what is right. There is no teaching of original sin or even actual sin in Daoism or Confucianism. Although they may need some instruction, humans are quite capable of completely following the *Dao* toward immortality.)

Responding to Confucianism and Daoism

Thinking in terms of Law and Gospel and sin and salvation, ask students *What do you think might be the biggest stumbling block to the Gospel for someone with Daoist or Confucian beliefs?* (Answers will vary. The cross will always be a stumbling block, but it is important to point out that those who do not recognize their need for salvation, have no use for a Savior. So,

along with sharing the Gospel, it is oftentimes necessary, when reaching out to non-Christians, to talk about the reality of sin, the inevitability of death, and the deceptions of the devil.)

There is an additional approach one might take. Have someone in the class read John 14:1–7. Then ask the class to share how this passage provides some insight into how to approach someone with Confucian or Daoist beliefs. Points to highlight are

- Humankind ultimately has an eternal destination. It will either be spent in blessedness with God or in torment with the devil.

- There are many people who have taught different ways to eternal life. Jesus taught that He was the only way.

Reiterate that Confucianism and Daoism do not recognize humankind's need for a Savior. *How might you give a reason to such a person for why he or she should consider the claims of Christ?* (Answers may vary, but emphasis should be placed on the resurrection of Christ [without intitally even mentioning His deity]. By dying and rising, Jesus is in the best position to speak authoritatively about the blessed destination of humankind and the *way* to get there.)

Closing

Conclude class with the following prayer:

Father, we thank You for sending Your eternal Son, because by His death and resurrection You have provided a way for all of humankind to live eternally with You. We ask that You increase in us true faith that Jesus' suffering, death, and resurrection was for each and every one of us. Help us also to be able to share this tremendous message of hope with our neighbors and friends, whoever they may be. Thank You for all You give us, and thank You for Your mercy. In Your name we pray. Amen.

8
CONFUCIANISM AND DAOISM

Understanding Confucianism and Daoism

History and Teachings

Confucianism and Daoism both emerged in ancient China. Around 500 BC, various feudal lords were locked in political and military conflict. This is known as the period of the Warring States. In the aftermath of the turmoil, many people began to ask how China could become reunited. Solutions were proposed by hundreds of intellectuals during the period of the Hundred Schools.

By far the two most influential thinkers were Confucius and Laozi. They both taught (in their respective writings—the *Analects of Confucius* and the *Dao de jing*) that the only way for society to recover from political and social devastation was for Chinese society to realign itself with the *Dao*, the way or path in which the universe was moving. However, they also taught two different ways of achieving harmony with the *Dao*.

Confucius claimed that harmony with the *Dao* was best attained by restoring order in society. Confucianism sees the family as the bedrock of society. Therefore, proper relationships at home between children, parents, grandparents, and even deceased ancestors (by veneration) needed to be instituted. Such order should also be found in society at large. Authorities are to be respected and obeyed, but authorities are also to recognize they have an obligation to their subjects. Recognizing such would bring society back on track and in alignment with the *Dao*.

Laozi taught differently. Laozi focused not on society but on nature. Nature, he taught, contained five elements—metal, earth, wood, fire, and water. Furthermore, it was empowered by two energies—yin (male) and yang (female). Harmony with the *Dao* and even immortality could be achieved by balancing the elements and energies. One might even be able to tap into the hidden and mysterious powers of the universe through meditation and contemplation. But ultimately, the goal is proper balance to achieve eternal life.

Confucianism and Daoism are not mutually exclusive. Today many Chinese embrace the teachings of Confucius as their ethical code of conduct and the mysterious notions of Daoism in their private, meditative life. How many is unclear, but it is surely also to be found throughout the large population of Asian Americans.

Responding to Confucianism and Daoism

Read **John 14:1–7.** How might this passage provide some insight into how one could approach someone with Confucian or Daoist beliefs?

9

Mormonism

THE CHURCH OF JESUS CHRIST OF LATTER-DAY SAINTS

Lesson Focus

The Church of Jesus Christ of Latter-day Saints is well-known for its high moral stance and strong emphasis on the family. Lesser known are many of the unique or unusual teachings surrounding this religious body. As Christians, we need to understand what the Latter-day Saints really teach and how we can share the true message of Christ with LDS followers.

Opening Discussion

Welcome your students as they arrive. Explain that the religious body you will be studying this session is The Church of Jesus Christ of Latter-day Saints (LDS), often called the Mormons. Many people assume the LDS to be a Christian religion. But as will become clear in this study, despite the LDS's own claim of falling within the umbrella of Christianity, The Church of Jesus Christ of Latter-day Saints is really a cult.

Ask the class to explain what they think is meant by "cult." (Student answers may vary; most may associate cults with "brainwashing" or otherwise manipulating their followers.) Then explain that a cult usually has the following characteristics:

1. Cults deny some or numerous parts of the Bible's teachings on the person and work of Christ. Their doctrine fails to correspond to the teachings of the Bible.

2. Cults have a leader or prophet who claims to have been inspired either to add to the teachings of the Bible or to supersede the teachings of the Bible.

3. Cults have unique and oftentimes peculiar secret rituals.

4. Cults apply their own unique definitions to standard Christian terminology.

5. Cults reject the historical Christian Church as totally corrupt.

Before going further in the session, say the following prayer:

Dear heavenly Father, sometimes it is easy for us to believe in things that only appear to be real. At times, something may look so good that we want to believe in it simply because it is outwardly appealing. Help us examine all spiritual things in the light of Your Word, so that we may always find the truth. We ask for Your blessings on our time together. Help us be open and honest with each other, and help us see things through Your eyes. We ask this in Jesus' name. Amen.

Understanding the Latter-day Saints

Distribute copies of Participant Page 9, found at the end of this study. Have students review the history and teachings of The Church of Jesus Christ of Latter-day Saints. Ask the students what they found especially striking about Mormonism. Be prepared to speak about the following aspects of Mormon doctrines:

Progressive revelation—The head of the LDS church is understood to be a "living prophet" in Mormonism. He can introduce new teachings. If these new teachings contradict earlier ones, the contradiction is explained by appealing to the concept of progressive revelation. The LDS claims God recognizes that the context in which Mormons live changes and thus church teachings change to fit new contexts.

Multiple sources of authority—Mormons maintain the following sources as foundational texts: *Doctrines and Covenants*; *The Pearl of Great Price*; *The Book of Mormon*; and the King James translation of the Bible (insofar as it is interpreted correctly).

God was once a man like we are—According to Mormon doctrine, Jesus, like God before Him, was born of His Father. Later He was reborn through a man and a woman. Through obedience, He earned His way to the celestial kingdom and godhood, taking His wives with Him.

We can become gods—Just like God before us, we can become a god through our good works. If you do well, you are placed in celestial heaven and can work your way up to godhood.

Heaven(s)—There are three heavens in Mormonism. Celestial heaven is for those Mormons who do enough good works on earth. Terrestrial heaven is for those who don't do well or are honorable non-Mormons. Telestial heaven is for those who are wicked.

After reviewing these LDS teachings, allow students to work alone or in pairs to look up the suggested Scripture verses that respond to these false beliefs. Summarize their findings with the whole group.

Progressive revelation—Matthew 5:17–19 (Christ has come to fulfill the Law, not to abolish it. Until heaven and earth come to an end, "not an iota, not a dot, will pass from the Law" [v. 18]. Those who attempt to relax or change the Word will become least in the kingdom of heaven.)

Multiple sources of authority—Revelation 22:18–19 (Those who try to add to or take away from the Word of God will suffer the plagues described in Scripture and/or lose the blessings described there.)

God was once a man like we are—Numbers 23:19; Psalm 90:2; Acts 12:21–23 ("God is not man . . . or a son of man" [Numbers 23:19]. God has existed since before the beginning of the world. He is "from everlasting to everlasting" [Psalm 90:2]. Those who claim to be God will be punished.)

We can become gods—Genesis 3:1–6, 22–24 (The concept of becoming like God is the very lie that Satan used to entice Adam and Eve into sin. When humankind tried to do this, God punished them and cut them off from the tree of life so we could not live forever in our sin.)

Heaven(s)—John 5:28–29; John 17:24–25 (We will rise and be judged to be with Christ or to suffer eternal punishment. We go to be with Christ where He is [in heaven] to see Him in His glory.)

Responding to the Latter-day Saints

After reading the fact sheet and contrasting Mormon doctrine with biblical doctrine, have the students read Galatians 1:6–9 and discuss the following questions:

What does St. Paul mean by "a different gospel"? (It is something other than the truth taken directly from the Word of God as preached by Jesus Christ and His apostles. Point out that the Gospel of Christ has never changed. Preaching and teaching may use a variety of words, but the content remains the same.)

How does Mormonism teach a different gospel? (Based on your discussion in the previous section, students should respond that the LDS teaches a gospel other than that given by Jesus and the apostles.)

Christians will encounter Mormons in the workplace, in schools, and in every avenue of life. There are three biblical suggestions that must be kept in mind when approaching a Mormon. Have individuals read the three passages found on the Participant Page and explain what instruction they offer:

1 Peter 3:15—Speak with them in love.

Romans 1:16–17; 10:14–15—Share the Gospel and the love Jesus has shown in your own life.

1 John 2:24—Don't let a Mormon lead you astray.

Closing

Conclude with the following prayer:

Dear Lord, we thank You for this time together. Thank You for allowing us to learn about other religions so that we might be better equipped to approach and respond to them in love for the truth of the Gospel. We know that You want all people to be saved. Help us by Your Spirit to witness to Your love with our voices and our lives. We ask this in Jesus' name. Amen.

9
MORMONISM
THE CHURCH OF JESUS CHRIST OF LATTER-DAY SAINTS

Understanding the Latter-day Saints

History and Teachings

The Church of Jesus Christ of Latter-day Saints was begun by Joseph Smith Jr. in 1830. Smith claimed to have translated the *Book of Mormon*, a primary source of their teachings, from golden tablets he uncovered in the woods of upstate New York after being visited by an angel named Moroni. Smith took his new religion to a series of locations from Ohio to Missouri. He finally founded his own community in Nauvoo, Illinois, where the church had its own laws and ordinances.

Their practices, especially polygamy, and unorthodox theology resulted in the persecution of the Mormon community. By 1844, Joseph Smith wound up in prison, where a mob attacked and killed him. To avoid further persecution, Smith's successor, Brigham Young, moved the group to the Salt Lake Valley in Utah, where they flourished. Mormon tabernacles have been erected in all parts of the United States and are under construction or planned for all major continents. There are around thirteen million Mormons in the world. More than five million live in the United States.

Many people mistake Mormonism for a Christian denomination. This is a gross misunderstanding. Mormons do not believe in the Trinity. Instead, they believe that the Bible teaches that there are three gods who are "united in love and purpose." One of its very peculiar and central teachings is that God was once a human being just like us and that, like God, we, too, can become gods and earn admittance into a celestial heaven. To reach the celestial kingdom, you must believe that Smith and his successor are true prophets, be baptized a Mormon, live a good life, obtain a celestial marriage, bear many children, attend all church functions, and pay tithes to the church. Mormons may not drink alcohol or hot beverages. They must not use tobacco and must observe many other strict practices.

Two early teachings of Mormonism that are especially startling are the exclusion of African Americans from the celestial heavens and that one is permitted to have numerous wives. Both these teachings have been overturned. How is this possible, especially when they believe that God revealed these things through Joseph Smith? Mormon doctrine includes the idea of progressive revelation. The most recent revelations of the current living prophet supersede or abrogate previous doctrines in their authoritative writings. In other words, doctrines can change. This makes Mormon doctrine tough to nail down. Nevertheless, it clearly contradicts the essential doctrines of Christianity.

Progressive revelation—**Matthew 5:17–19**

Multiple sources of authority—**Revelation 22:18–19**

God was once a man like we are—**Numbers 23:19**; **Psalm 90:2**; **Acts 12:21–23**

We can become gods—**Genesis 3:1–6, 22–24**

Heaven(s)—**John 5:28–29; 17:24–25**

Responding to the Latter-day Saints

Read **Galatians 1:6–9**. What does St. Paul mean by "a different gospel"?

How does Mormonism teach a different gospel?

1 Peter 3:15

Romans 1:16–17; 10:14–15

1 John 2:24

 Participant Page 9 *One God, many gods* © 2008 Concordia Publishing House. Scripture: ESV™. Reproduced by permission.

10
Jehovah's Witnesses

Lesson Focus

Jehovah's Witnesses have a zeal for sharing their beliefs that puts most Christians to shame. Unfortunately, even though they use the name *Jehovah*, this is a cult and not a Christian church.

Opening Discussion

Have you ever been part of or witnessed a conversation between a Christian and a Jehovah's Witness? (Answers will vary; many students may have had this experience.) *What do you know about Jehovah's Witnesses?* (The level of student knowledge is probably very low.) Inform students that while Jehovah's Witnesses are a cult, they are growing gradually in number, primarily because of their prosely-tizing zeal.

Begin the study with the following prayer:

Dearest Jesus, You came to earth as both true God and true man to pay for the sins of all people. There is no other way to heaven except through You. As we study Jehovah's Witnesses, give us words that will help us to tell others about salvation through You. We ask this in Your name. Amen.

Understanding Jehovah's Witnesses

Distribute copies of Participant Page 10, which covers the history and teachings of Jehovah's Witnesses. Ask the students to read and then discuss their impressions of Jehovah's Witnesses.

Be prepared to answer questions about the history of Jehovah's Witnesses. The following may be helpful. Charles T. Russell was origi-nally a pastor of a small-group Bible study in Pittsburgh at the age of eighteen. He had no for-mal theological training. Nevertheless, he was able to command the obedience of numerous people. And now, despite their manifest contra-dictions of Scripture, Jehovah's Witnesses have blossomed into a massive worldwide organiza-tion.

In addition to the brief statement of their teachings on the Participant Page, Jehovah's Witnesses also teach that God created human-kind and gave Satan temporary dominion over the earth in order to prove that His human creations could remain faithful and obedient to Him. According to the Witnesses, Jesus—who is not God but just a created spiritual being (the archangel Michael) before and after He was on earth and only a human being while on earth—began His second coming and Jehovah's everlasting kingdom on earth in 1914. As a result of His second coming, Satan's dominion will soon be destroyed and God's government will be established.

Jehovah's Witnesses also do not believe in hell. Those who do not do enough good deeds (primarily by proselytizing) will simply cease to exist when they die.

It should be noted that Jehovah's Witnesses do not question the teachings of *The Watchtower,* the periodical published by their national offices. The church leaders at their national offices in Brooklyn wield a tremendous amount of power.

Responding to Jehovah's Witnesses

Stress to the students how Jehovah's Witnesses divert attention away from the historical and biblical person and work of Christ by emphasizing the following teachings:

Christ was sacrificed only as a human being. Ask the students to respond after reading Colossians 2:9 and 1 Peter 2:24. (The full deity of God was in the person of Christ. Christ Himself bore our sins on the cross.)

Christ sacrificed His human body only for Adam. Ask the students to respond after reading Romans 6:8–11. (Christ died on the cross so that we might *all* die and rise with Him.)

One is saved through his or her own works. Ask the students to respond after reading Ephesians 2:8–9; Romans 3:24; and 1 John 1:7. (We are saved by grace through faith, not as a result of our works. We are justified as a gift of grace through Jesus Christ. The blood of Christ cleanses us from sin.)

One can never be certain of his or her salvation. Ask the students to respond after reading John 3:36; 5:24; and 1 John 5:13. ("Whoever believes in the Son has eternal life" [John 3:36]. Those who believe will not come into judgment but have eternal life: "that you may know that you have eternal life" [1 John 5:13].)

Explain to the students that God's Word urges us to testify to the truth as witnesses to Jesus. While sharing your faith with a Jehovah's Witness may make you uncomfortable, such conversations, particularly when they point to the person and work of Christ, are the means through which the Holy Spirit works. So one should never shy away from or hide from the Jehovah's Witness that may show up on your doorstep. However, students should also know that Jehovah's Witnesses are well-trained and often ready to respond to Christian arguments. If time allows, you may want to offer practical suggestions for conversing with a Jehovah's Witness as detailed in *How to Respond: Jehovah's Witnesses* (CPH item #12-6005).

Closing

Conclude with the following prayer:

Dear God, You are the Father, the Son, and the Holy Spirit. Teach us how to witness to Jehovah's Witnesses so that they may be rescued from their sins, just as we also have been rescued from ours through Jesus Christ, our Lord. Give us the words to speak and the compassion to overcome their false teachings with Your Word and Your Spirit. Thank You for the wonderful free gift of our salvation through Jesus, and forgive us when we take that gift for granted. Help us be prepared to testify to You at all times. In Jesus' name we pray. Amen.

10

JEHOVAH'S WITNESSES

Understanding Jehovah's Witnesses

History and Teachings

The roots of Jehovah's Witnesses are found in the late nineteenth and early twentieth centuries. They begin with Charles T. Russell (1852–1916), who founded *The Watchtower Bible and Tract Society* in 1884. A few years later, he published *Zion's Watchtower*, which outlined his novel interpretation of the Bible. The group that eventually formed around his teachings was officially called Jehovah's Witnesses in 1931. Under the leadership of Russell's successor, Joseph F. Rutherford, the organization was incorporated in Brooklyn, New York, where a small group of men continue to this day to direct the work and determine the teachings of the Witnesses. Today, Jehovah's Witnesses is an international organization with membership of nearly seven million people.

Jehovah's Witnesses are an apocalyptic religious community. They believe that they were organized to announce the early establishment of God's kingdom on earth. But they also have some other peculiar interpretations of Scripture, found in their *Watchtower* magazines, which contradict clear biblical teachings.

Jehovah's Witnesses believe that Adam was created to be perfect, but when he sinned, he lost the right of eternal life for all of his offspring, that is, the whole world. Jesus Christ, who is the "created" Son of God (but not God Himself), was sent to earth to be a perfect and blameless human to pay for Adam's sin. This does not save us but opens the door for us to prove our worthiness. The Witnesses deny hell and claim that only 144,000 will be in heaven while the rest of the faithful will be on the new earth. They also believe that they are called to gather the other "sheep," thus earning their place on the new earth. You will most likely encounter Jehovah's Witnesses at your own doorstep at some time or another. Door-to-door witnessing is the primary activity and duty of a Jehovah's Witness.

Responding to Jehovah's Witnesses

Christ was sacrificed only as a human being. **Colossians 2:9; 1 Peter 2:24**

Christ sacrificed His human body only for Adam. **Romans 6:8–11**

One is saved through his or her own works. **Ephesians 2:8–9; Romans 3:24; 1 John 1:7**

One can never be certain of his or her salvation. **John 3:36; 5:24; 1 John 5:13**

11

Scientology

Lesson Focus

Scientology has attracted a fair number of prominent big-screen stars, some of whom have become very outspoken about their beliefs and practices. Through this session, students will explore some of the history and basic teachings of Scientology as well as the truth found in God's Word.

Opening Discussion

Ask, *What do you know or have you heard about Scientology? Who are some more well-known Scientologists?* (Students are more likely to know the names of celebrity Scientologists such as Tom Cruise and John Travolta than they are to be aware of specific Scientologist teachings. What little they do know may relate to secret and unusual Scientology practices or "audits.")

After a brief discussion, begin the class with the following prayer:

> *Heavenly Father, to those who don't know You, Your promises may seem too good to be true. Today, as we look at some of the empty promises of false religion, give us a renewed joy in knowing the truth of Your promises. We especially praise You for the promise fulfilled in the coming Your Son, Jesus Christ, to save our world from sin. Make us witnesses of this Good News to all whose hearts long for a promise that is true. In Jesus' name we pray. Amen.*

Understanding Scientology

Provide copies of Participant Page 11, and have students review the history and teachings of Scientology. Explain to the group that Scientology is a relatively new religion founded by a man named L. Ron Hubbard in 1954. Hubbard was a novelist. Many of the terms that Scientologists use sound like something out of a science fiction novel.

Have the class compare and contrast the teachings of Scientology listed on the Participant Page with the corresponding Bible passages.

Human nature is good. Compare with Psalm 51:5 and Romans 3:12. (We are conceived and born in sin. "No one does good, not even one" [Romans 3:12].)

Truth is found within, once one overcomes his or her engrams. Compare with John 8:31–32 and John 14:6. (Only through Christ do we have the truth. He is the way and the truth and the life.)

The root of human problems is our ignorance of ourselves and our true nature. Compare with Genesis 3:16–19; Romans 5:12; and Galatians 6:7–8. (Our root problem is sin and the punishment brought upon all of creation as a result of sin. The progression from sin to death has spread to all humankind as the result of one sin. What we sow, we also reap.)

The answer to our problems is found in self-discovery through the process of auditing. Compare with John 16:33; Acts 4:12; Romans 8:31, 35, 37–39; and 1 Peter 5:7. (We overcome the world through faith in Christ. There is salvation in no one except Christ. Nothing can separate us from the love of God in Christ Jesus. We can put all our cares and anxieties on Christ.)

Responding to Scientology

Explain to the class that even though Scientology uses very bizarre terminology, it still attracts a lot of followers. Ask them what they think are the reasons for the attraction to Scientology.

Scientology seems to offer the promise of a happy, problem-free life and the chance for immortality. Explain to the class how this is attractive to people who are experiencing emptiness in their lives. People who are lonely or burdened by some kind of trouble and are anxious for answers are vulnerable to the claims of Scientology. Possibly the greatest appeal of Scientology is that it is something you can do for yourself. If you pay the money and take the courses on auditing, it promises to teach you methods to unlock the hidden potential within yourself. It promises control of your own life. This is appealing to people who feel as if they are living in a world that is out of control.

Explain to the class that Scientology rarely refers to Jesus. When it does, it describes Him and His death on the cross as a mere symbol of the potential triumph of the immortal spirit

over the body. Have students look up the Bible passages listed in this section of the Participant Page. How might the words of these passages be used to provide hope to a person who feels helpless and in need of answers to life's big questions?

Matthew 1:21 (Christ was born to save His people from their sins. This includes all who believe in Him.)

Matthew 16:15–16 (Simon Peter testifies to the true identity of Jesus. He is "the Christ, the Son of the living God." Jesus is not just a great teacher or prophet but the very Son of God come to earth to save us.)

Mark 1:9–11 (The Father in heaven acknowledges Jesus as His only beloved Son. Christ does not rely on His own claims as Son; the Father, Himself, acknowledges the same thing.)

John 11:25–26 (In Christ we have the assurance of the resurrection.)

Closing

Conclude this study with the following prayer:

Lord, so many people in our world are looking for happiness and salvation. We thank You Lord that we belong to You and that we know Your awesome love for us and Your promise of salvation. Today we pray for all those people who are struggling in any way. We pray that they would not be taken in by empty promises that are too good to be true. We pray that they would not rely on themselves and find despair but turn to You and find hope. Lord, we especially pray for these people that we silently mention in our hearts. (Observe a time of silence.) Be with them whatever their needs are, and use us to speak Your Good News to them. In Jesus' name we pray. Amen.

11

SCIENTOLOGY

Understanding Scientology

History and Teachings

Scientology is a very new cult. It was founded by the novelist L. Ron Hubbard (1911–1986) with the publication of his book, *Dianetics: The Modern Science of Mental Health.* Other writings by Hubbard are widely available in bookstores and other places where books are sold. *Dianetics* is usually marketed as a self-help book. Possibly the greatest exposure for Scientology comes through the endorsement of its celebrity members, who donate money and make appearances on behalf of the church. Tom Cruise is probably the most famous Scientologist today, although other notable celebrities such as John Travolta, Kirstie Alley, and Lisa Marie Presley are or have at one time been involved in the organization.

The basic teaching of Scientology is that human beings can, by raising their own spiritual awareness, achieve immortality. Human beings are basically good and capable of discovering spiritual truths by themselves. What holds people back is not sin but a lack of awareness about our selves and our surroundings, which causes illnesses and general unhappiness.

Students of Scientology are called *preclears.* Through a process known as *auditing*, which is said to clear the mind of *engrams* (negative mental images), preclears work toward reaching a state of absolute mental and spiritual clarity. Through the lengthy (and expensive) process of auditing, preclears hope to reach this level of spiritual awareness and immortality. Once this stage is attained, the Scientologist is called an *operating thetan.*

Human nature is good. Compare with **Psalm 51:5** and **Romans 3:12**.

Truth is found within, once one overcomes his or her engrams. Compare with **John 8:31–32** and **14:6**.

The root of human problems is our ignorance of ourselves and our true nature. Compare with **Genesis 3:16–19**; **Romans 5:12**; and **Galatians 6:7–8**.

The answer to our problems is found in self-discovery through the process of auditing. Compare with **John 16:33**; **Acts 4:12**; **Romans 8:31, 35, 37–39**; and **1 Peter 5:7**.

Responding to Scientology

How might the words of these passages be used to provide hope to a person who feels helpless and in need of answers to life's big questions?

Matthew 1:21

Matthew 16:15–16

Mark 1:9–11

John 11:25–26

12
The New Age

Lesson Focus

Students may not be as familiar with the New Age movement as they are with other religious groups, in part because New Age thinking has become so much a part of daily life in the twenty-first century. Through this lesson, you will expose the darkness of the New Age to the light of God's Word.

Opening Discussion

Begin by explaining to the class that today's topic is going to cover a religious philosophy that offers a new way of handling the old problem of sin. After identifying it as the New Age movement, ask the class what they know about the New Age. Students may have difficulty defining the New Age movement, since it has become somewhat mainstream in the last twenty years.

Before moving on, offer the following prayer:

Father, thank You for being a tried-and-true God whom we can depend on in all our struggles. Help us examine all things, old and new, with Your wisdom and truth. May the light of our Savior, Jesus Christ, continue to shine into the dark and confusing areas of our lives. We ask this in His name. Amen.

Understanding New Age

Provide copies of Participant Page 12 and direct students to the history and teachings of the New Age. After the students have had some time to look over it, emphasize the following points:

- The New Age movement does not reject any religion or philosophy. It teaches that that whatever feels right to you is right for you.

- New Age followers do not believe in or even love God. They believe they are gods themselves.

- New Age followers will often use concepts that are familiar to Christians but assign them new meanings. For example, when the Bible asserts that those who trust in Jesus are "born again," New Age thinkers understand this as reincarnation.

- New Age influences in society are rarely obvious. Much that is described as self-help and motivational is really New Age in its philosophy.

After explaining how important it is for Christians to be able to identify New Age philosophies, discuss the following obvious markers of New Age:

- The use of chants—songs or recitations repeated over and over again to encourage inward focus for meditation
- The use of crystals—natural rock or stone formations that are used to aid in healing physical ailments or treated as a source of power
- Mind-altering drugs—use of LSD, marijuana, and other chemicals to produce altered states of consciousness to increase spiritual awareness
- Faith in self—claims that we are our own best source of provision, healing, and restoration
- Hypnosis—achieving psychically induced states that leave the mind open to external manipulation
- Ouija boards—a tool said to be used for communicating with the spirit world
- Psychics—people who claim to have cosmic power, energy, or insight
- Relativism—a philosophy denying absolute standards or values
- Spirit guides—consulting or communicating with a nonphysical personality who communicates through a medium or channel
- Tarot cards—a deck of cards that are believed to be able to reveal the secrets of the universe

Responding to New Age

Draw attention to the New Age quest for knowledge and realization. Ask, *Where does the New Age always directs its attention?* (It's always directed toward the internal and the hidden and mysterious.)

Have a student read 1 John 2:20–25. Ask the reader or someone else to explain what this passage means. Emphasize that this section of Scripture is addressing its reader as one who has access to the very revelation of God. It reminds us that the Holy Spirit is at work in us and that we have the truth of God's very Word to guide us in our quest for wisdom. It gives us the criteria for identifying false claims of knowledge of the divine (vv. 22–23). It also reminds us that the truth about Jesus has been around since the beginning and has stood the test of time, and it commands and motivates us to abide in this eternal truth.

Next, ask the class to identify some ways to combat subtle indoctrination of New Age thought. Be sure to include these in the list:

Dedicate time to Bible study, acknowledging the truth according to God's Word.

Make use of the blessings given us in Holy Communion.

Trust in God for all things.

Be in fellowship with other Christians.

Be regular in our worship of the one, true God.

Pray to the one, true God through Jesus Christ.

Repent (a change of mind to obediently listen to and heed God's Word).

Closing

Conclude by reminding the class that the New Age movement isn't really new. Since the Garden of Eden, Satan has been tempting us to be our own god. Invite the class to join in a circle prayer asking God for forgiveness for the times we let Satan trick us into being our own god, for protection from Satan's evil schemes, and for wisdom to better recognize God's truth. Conclude with the following: *Lord, we ask these things in the name of our Lord and Savior—Your Son, Jesus Christ. Amen.*

12
THE NEW AGE

Understanding the New Age

History and Teachings

The New Age movement is a blend of many Eastern religious concepts. It has no specific leader, no special head-quarters, and claims no sacred writings as its own. The New Age movement does not even consistently identify itself as a religion. It might best be described as a loose network of organizations and individuals who believe that human-kind can and must "fix" themselves and the world through enlightened thinking. Its beliefs come mainly from the vari-ous Eastern religions (Hinduism, Buddhism, and others), the occult (magic, astrology, tarot cards, and various other prac-tices), and distortions of Christianity.

New Age adopts the deities, founders, and prophets of several other religions as spiritual role models. Jesus, for example, is one of the many "ascended masters"—people who recognized their divine capabilities and used them. Other significant figures of the New Age movement are celebrities such as actress Shirley MacLaine, the late folk artist John Denver, Deepak Chopra, and even to some extent Oprah Winfrey. The association of celebrities with the New Age movement tends to give it an air of credibility.

New Age influence is subtle but pervasive. Its influence can be seen in modern self-help movements (TM, yoga, and Zen), in school curricula (secular humanism), in popular music styles (New Age music), and in the themes of many movies and television programs (from *Star Wars* to *The Matrix*).

Despite its many variations, New Age followers generally advocate personal and social transformation through self-development, cosmic evolution, spiritism, and political activ-ism. According to New Age thought, the primary reason for social problems and disharmony is our failure to realize our unlimited personal potential.

Other major teachings among New Age gurus include espe-cially a general belief in monism. Everything is God; God is not a person but an impersonal con-sciousness or force found in everything. The New Age move-ment seeks to help people discover the deity within through various spiritual exercises and therapies. Christ is not a person but a posi-tion, a level of "divine conscious-ness" that anyone can attain. The movement encourages toleration, rejects absolutes, and embraces all forms of spiritual striving including reincarnation, *karma*, channeling (communicating with gods, spirits, and the souls of the dead through mediums), psychic healing, and enlightened "Christ-consciousness."

13
Satanism

Lesson Focus

The study of satanism may bring to mind images of teens dabbling in occult rituals or worshipers dressed in hooded black robes while making blood sacrifice. The spiritual reality for those who practice satanism is even darker.

Opening Discussion

After informing the class that the topic for discussion in the current session is satanism, ask them to offer their impressions of satanism. The very term *satanism* will probably evoke fear. Rather than avoiding or hiding from the horrendous evil of satanism, emphasize that all non-Christian religions are aberrations of the devil. Thus, like the other religions of the world, satanism too must be understood and responded to by Christians.

You may also want to discuss what it is about satanism that draws people to it, especially teenagers. Let the class offer its opinions. Explain that specialists in the occult and satanism typically say that many are drawn into satanism in search of power. So they seek out black magic and other secret occult rituals. Still others are drawn to satanism because it appeals to our sinful instincts. For example, rather than teaching one to turn the other cheek, satanism teaches that one should respond to violence with violence.

Before studying the history and teachings of satanism, say the following prayer:

Heavenly Father, You are the God of truth, and You have revealed that truth to us through Your Word and through Jesus Christ. Send Your Holy Spirit among us now as we study the deception of satanism, and chase Satan away from us. Help us to resist him, so that we will not be easily fooled by his lies. Forgive us when we sin, bless us as Your children, and free us from the power of sin, death, and the devil through the work of Your Son, our Savior, Jesus. In His name we pray. Amen.

Understanding Satanism

Distribute copies of Participant Page 13, and have students review the teachings of satanism found at the end of this study. After the class has a chance to read and consider this information, ask them again what they think is the biggest draw to satanism.

Read 2 Corinthians 4:4 and John 8:44, and then discuss the following questions:

Why does satanism continue to exist? (Satan will exist in this world until the final judgment. His goal is to blind people so that they do not see the truth and to deceive them about God's gracious love.)

Why do people who worship Satan believe they are right? (Their minds are clouded. They believe what they want to believe, not the truths revealed in Scripture.)

Why can we trust in God and not Satan? (There is no truth in Satan. He is a liar and a deceiver and tells people what they want to hear. God's Word is the truth, and He is honest with everyone, even though this is, at times, much harder to hear than Satan's message of power and self-indulgence.)

What is most dangerous about Satan? (He is a deceiver. He makes people think they do not need a Savior.)

In concluding this section, make the following points:

- Satan has been attacking God's people since Adam and Eve were created. His tactics have not changed because human beings have not changed. Humans are still sinful and selfish.

- Satan uses our sinful nature to lure people away from God and into his domain.

- Satan uses the sin he committed to lure others into worshiping him. Satan wanted to be like God himself and was thrown out of heaven by God to roam the earth (Revelation 2:7–9).

- Satan knows that humans also want to be more like God, knowing the difference between good and evil and having power over life. With this in mind, the devil has become an expert recruiter for turning God's people away from Him.

Responding to Satanism

Ask, *What is the best response to Satan and satanism?* (Student answers will vary.) After the discussion, have the class read Matthew 4:1–11 and answer the question again. Emphasize that only God's Word can overcome Satan. It is therefore vital that Christians be thoroughly acquainted with the teachings of the Bible, not just in dealing with satanism, but in their dealings with anything, for all our struggles are ultimately against Satan (Ephesians 6:12).

Have the class read the Bible passages listed on the Participant Page and summarize their content.

John 8:44—Satan is the father of lies.

2 Corinthians 11:3—We are often deceived by Satan (and we do not even know it).

1 Corinthians 15:55–57—Christ is and will be victorious over Satan.

Colossians 1:13–14—Christ will protect us from Satan's attacks.

James 4:7—Through Christ's strength alone can we make Satan flee.

1 John 4:4—Christ has overcome he who is in the world (Satan).

Closing

Conclude with the following prayer:

Dear Lord Jesus Christ, You defeated Satan when You took our sins upon Yourself and gave up Your life for us on the cross. You defeated his reign of power when You rose from the dead to conquer death for us. Please hold us in Your truth, Lord, so that we might not be so easily deceived by Satan. Keep us rooted in Your Word and guide our paths away from the evil one. Help us live lives that glorify You and find real joy in Your truth. In Your name we pray. Amen.

13
SATANISM

Understanding Satanism

History and Teachings

There is no unified organization or set of teachings associated with modern Satanism. There are, however, two historical persons typically associated with the movement. Aleister Crowley (1875–1947) founded the British satanic group known as the *Ordo Templi Orientis* after experimenting with the occult beginning when he was in his twenties. His writings exerted a great deal of influence upon Anton LaVey (1930–1997), who wrote *The Satanic Bible* and *The Satanic Rituals* and founded the International Church of Satan.

Traditional Satanism emphasizes worship of a powerful, personal devil through cultic ritual and black magic. This form has not disappeared. But modern Satanists frequently reject the worship of Satan. Instead, they advocate that everyone indulge in whatever activity they want, without limit or restraint.

The Church of Satan follows these guidelines for behavior:

- Prayer is useless. It distracts people from useful activity.

- Enjoy indulgence instead of abstinence. Practice with joy the seven deadly sins—greed, pride, envy, anger, gluttony, lust, and sloth.

- If someone smites you on one cheek, smash him on the other.

- Do unto others as they do unto you.

- Engage in sexual activity freely in accordance with your desires and needs.

- Suicide is frowned upon.

- Man is just another animal—the most vicious of all.

- A Satanist is not bound to any rules.

Essentially, what Satanism attempts to accomplish is to overturn what God teaches in the Scriptures. It sees the teachings of Scripture as reinforcing weakness and failing to teach self-reliance and the pursuit of pleasure.

Responding to Satanism

John 8:44

2 Corinthians 11:3

1 Corinthians 15:55–57

Colossians 1:13–14

James 4:7

1 John 4:4

14

Rastafarianism

Lesson Focus

Most students may be well-acquainted with the sounds of reggae music but have little or no knowledge of the religious practice of Rastafarianism, which greatly influences reggae.

Opening Discussion

Begin by asking the class what religion they think of when they hear reggae music or see someone with dreadlocks. If anyone answers that it is Rastafarianism, ask them to explain what they know of it and how they came to learn about it. If no one knows about it, explain that the topic will be a very new religion that emerged in Jamaica just after a man named Ras Tafari Makonnen became Emperor Haile Selassie of Ethiopia in 1930. Ask them again if they might know what the topic for the session might be. If students have not yet figured out which group you are studying this week, share with them that today's topic will be Rastafarianism.

Understanding Rastafarianism

Distribute copies of Participant Page 14 and review the history and teachings of Rastafarianism found there. As students review, ask for any questions they might have. Be prepared to discuss the basic beliefs of Rastafarianism. In addition to what is on the description page, L. P. Howell, an early preacher of Rastafarianism and founder of a settle-

ment in Kingston, Jamaica, included this list (the disbanding of this settlement would lead to their migration into the United States):

- A hatred of the "white race"
- Belief in the superiority of the "black race"
- Future revenge on the wicked of the "white race"
- Future defeat of the Jamaican government
- Preparation for returning to Africa
- Acknowledgement of the status of Emperor Selassie as the supreme being

Three important terms in Rastafarianism are *Babylon*—the white political power structure that Rastafarians are to make war against until its destruction;

I and I—concept of the unity of divinity found within everything (yet Selassie is paradoxically the supreme being);

Jah—Rastafarian word for God.

Ask the students how such a bizarre religion could be created. In light of Romans 1:18–25 and the turmoil of the times, it seems that it was crafted to provide a unifying ideology with divine pretension for the people of Jamaica.

Responding to Rastafarianism

In many ways, Rastafarianism as a religion seems to identify itself vis-à-vis Christianity, which Rastafarians (and the Nation of Islam) would call the white man's religion. Discuss ways in which a Christian could respond to this charge. (The kingdom of heaven is open to all who believe in Jesus Christ as Lord and Savior.)

In reality, Christianity is the religion for all people regardless of race, sex, social status, and so forth. Assign students one or more of the Bible verses listed on the Participant Page. Have them read the verse and decide what individuals or groups of people are considered part of God's kingdom by faith. Review their findings with the whole group.

Matthew 28:19—all nations

Galatians 3:27–28—Jew or Greek; slave and free; male or female

Acts 8:26–40—an Ethiopian official (assumed to be black)

Acts 2:39—all whom God calls to Himself

Acts 3:1–8—those who are sick or disabled

Acts 8:4–25—Samaritans (those of mixed blood) and those who formerly practiced satanic arts (magician)

Acts 10:1–45—Gentiles, specifically Romans, and military officers

Acts 13:6–12—those who had worshiped the devil and performed works in his name

Acts 16:11–15—a wealthy Gentile businesswoman

Acts 16:25–34—a jailer and his family

Acts 17:16–34—the intellectual elite

Acts 21:20—the Jews

1 Thessalonians 1:7–10—pagans and idol worshipers

Rastafarians do have some authoritative texts—the Holy Piby (also known as the black man's Bible). But the real authority and major figure is Selassie—the supreme being. Have students look up John 14:6 and discuss a Christian response to this claim. (The work of Christ, by virtue of His person, trumps Selassie.) This is the appropriate Christian response to Rastafarianism.

Closing

Conclude with the following prayer:

Dear heavenly Father, You sent Your Son to seek out and save the lost. He died so that the world might be reconciled to You. Give us the courage to proclaim this message to all who have not heard this message of total liberation. We ask this in the name of Your Son, who lives and reigns with You and the Holy Spirit. Amen.

14
RASTAFARIANISM

Understanding Rastafarianism

History and Teachings

Rastafarianism has its roots in a Black Nationalist movement begun by a Jamaican named Marcus Garvey (1887–1940). In 1927, he announced that in the future a leader would emerge from Africa who would deliver the black urban masses. Three years later, in Ethiopia, Ras Tafari Makonnen (1892–1975) was crowned Emperor Selassie and given the title "King of Kings, Lord of Lords, His Imperial Majesty of the Conquering Lion of the Tribe of Judah, Elect of God." He was seen by many Jamaicans as a great liberator of blacks, but eventually his admirers would identify him in messianic if not divine terms. A new religion was thus spawned, named Rastafarianism after the original name of Emperor Selassie.

Many of the founders of this new religion would wind up in the United States in the 1960s and '70s. They would be instrumental in providing the ideological backbone to the Black Nationalist movement in America. (This would eventually spawn the Nation of Islam, which shares many similarities with Rastafarianism.) There are probably about a million Rastafarians across the world today. Only about five thousand live in America.

Many Rastafarians believe Selassie is still alive today, and thus they acknowledge him as a supreme being. Rastafarianism (and even more so the Nation of Islam) asserts the superiority of what it calls the black race. Because whites are largely responsible for bringing blacks out of their African homeland to places in the West like Jamaica and the West Indies, Rastafarianism reserves a special hatred for the white race. It envisions a future where blacks will take their vengeance out on whites and return to the homeland of Ethiopia, where God (*Jah*) will rule over them in what will be a heaven on earth.

Rastafarians traditionally wear the colors of red, green, gold, and black. Red represents the blood of the martyrs, green the fauna of Ethiopia, and gold is to remind them to observe a strict moral code. This moral code demands that one not desecrate the body, keep from eating pork and shellfish, desire and strive to ultimately unite the world under the governance of *Jah*, and so on.

Some aspects of Rastafarianism are now making a comeback and have become popularized. This is primarily due the influence of reggae music. Dreadlocks and the consumption of marijuana—both part and parcel of Rastafarianism—are now part of popular culture.

Responding to Rastafarianism

According to these verses, who is included in God's kingdom by faith?

Matthew 28:19

Galatians 3:27–28

Acts 8:26–40

Acts 2:39

Acts 3:1–8

Acts 8:4–25

Acts 10:1–45

Acts 13:6–12

Acts 16:11–15

Acts 16:25–34

Acts 17:16–34

Acts 21:20

1 Thessalonians 1:7–10

15
Atheism

Lesson Focus

Atheists—along with agnostics and skeptics—want to deny the existence of God. They have suppressed the natural knowledge of God (Romans 1:19–20) and exchanged it for a lie. As Christians, we know God not only through our natural knowledge, but as He is revealed to us in Scripture.

Opening Discussion

Read the following parable:

While traveling through a forest, two hikers came upon an open field filled with many beautiful flowers arranged in neat rows. Yet, there were also many weeds. Some of the flowers were shriveled up, and many were dead. One hiker turned to his partner and said, "A gardener must tend this field." The other responded, "Nonsense." So they decided to wait, hiding in the shadows of the surrounding tree line, to see if a gardener ever showed up. They waited for weeks but never saw anyone arrive to tend to the flowers in the field. Yet, the hiker who believed a gardener existed persisted in his belief. The other hiker mocked him, saying: "Fine! Believe that a gardener exists! But you have to admit that we've never seen him and the evidence that he does exist is slim."

(Paraphrased from "Theology and Falsification," in *New Essays in Philosophical Theology* [London: SCM, 1955]).

Explain that parables like this are used by atheists or those who do not believe God exists to point out the futility of believing in God. Then ask students, *On the basis of what evidence do you believe God exists?* (This should spark some interesting conversation. It is one of the most important questions atheists ask. Let the students talk about it for some time, but keep the discussion on target.)

Conclude with the following prayer:

Heavenly Father, all of creation testifies to Your bountiful goodness! The heavens declare Your glory; the skies proclaim Your handiwork! But You have especially made Yourself known when You sent Your Son to die for our sins and rise for our salvation. Keep us ever mindful of this, especially when we are challenged with our own doubts and the doubts of others. Amen.

Understanding Atheism

Provide copies of Participant Page 15. Have students read through the history and teachings of atheism. Ask, *What do you think about the claims of atheism? What is the driving force of atheism?* (Many Christians claim that the only reason people become atheists is because they do not want to be accountable to God for their sin. This may be true for many atheists, but the public atheists, who are not grossly immoral, claim scientific reasons for their atheism. They just don't see that there is any good reason to believe in God's existence.)

There are several good scientific or philosophical arguments supporting the existence of God. Briefly explain the following two to the class.

The cosmological argument: Whatever begins to exist has a cause. The universe began to exist. Therefore, there is a cause behind the existence of the universe. That cause is God.

The moral argument: If God does not exist, universal and objective moral values and duties do not exist. Objective moral values and duties do exist. Therefore, God exists.

After explaining these and other arguments for God's existence that you may know of, ask the class to assess their strengths and weaknesses. You'll want to especially note that the God these arguments testify to is still a hidden and incompletely revealed God (see Acts 17:22–31).

Responding to Atheism

If arguments for God's existence are only helpful insofar as they point to the probability of the existence of God, then what would a particularly Christian response to atheism look like? Ask the students, *How would you respond to an atheist who asks you why you believe in God?* (Many will point to their faith that He exists. Others will argue that the Bible says He exists.) These are all legitimate responses within a Christian framework. But is there something else a Christian might suggest?

Referring back to the parable at the beginning of the chapter, suggest to the students that Christianity claims that the proverbial gardener did in fact make an appearance in the garden, in the person and work of Christ. This is Christianity's greatest response to the challenge of atheism: that God was in Christ (a historical person) reconciling the world unto Himself (2 Corinthians 5:19).

Take time to explore this idea or response to the claims of atheism. If you want to develop this particular Christian apologetic further, consider reading Craig Parton's *The Defense Never Rests* (CPH item 12-4190).

Closing

Conclude with the following prayer:

Heavenly Father, You loved us so much that You sent Your Son to die for us. Help us to reflect Your love to others and give us the courage to always be prepared to make a defense for the hope that is within us so that those who have rejected You may come to trust in You for their eternal salvation. Amen.

15
ATHEISM

Understanding Atheism

History and Teachings

Contemporary atheist author Richard Dawkins and several other contemporary writers such as Sam Harris and Christopher Hitchens have made quite a name for themselves. They have authored bestselling books with such startling titles as *The God Delusion*, *The End of Faith*, and *God Is Not Great*.

The media has dubbed them the "new atheists" even though atheism is actually quite old. Indeed, there must have been atheists around the time of King David, for he mentions them in Psalm 14. Nevertheless, the new atheism does have a slightly unique aspect to it. Its roots can be traced back to a contemporary philosophical movement known as logical positivism.

A. J. Ayer (1910–1989) was probably the most conspicuous member. In a work entitled *Language, Truth, and Logic* (1936), he claimed that when one states that such and such a thing exists, one is making a claim that is a matter of fact. It should then be verifiable by some sort of factual evidence. When it came to the claim "God exists," he was convinced there were no facts to support this. Thus, he concluded all talk about God is essentially meaningless gibberish.

Contemporary atheism has inherited this philosophical bias. But in addition to being convinced there is no evidence for God's existence, it also believes that in order for human civilization to progress, it must give up its religious beliefs. Therefore, most contemporary atheist writings were written to convince their readers to abandon their religion.

In addition to the more technical claim that to talk about God is meaningless because His existence is not empirically verifiable, there are other arguments atheists advance against belief in the existence of God. Some argue that the existence of natural and moral evils in the world is incompatible with the notion of an all-loving and all-powerful God. Others claim that God is a product of the human imagination, invented by more primitive people to account for the created order.

Quick Comparison Charts

Use the reproducible pages that follow for a
quick comparison between each of the religious
groups covered in *One God, many gods*.
The Web sites listed on each of these pages were active
at the time of publication. Concordia Publishing House
is not responsible for the content of these sites,
nor does it endorse them. The Ontario (Canada) Consultants
on Religious Tolerance provides an excellent general Web site
on world religions at www.religioustolerance.org.

CHRISTIANITY

History

The Christian Church dates its beginning from Pentecost in AD 30. The Church was essentially one body for a thousand years. A split between the East and West in 1054, the Reformation movement in the sixteenth century, and other divisions in the past five hundred years have resulted in hundreds of denominations today.

Central Teaching

Christians recognize Jesus to be the Christ (the Anointed One or Messiah) sent by God to redeem all people from sin. Jesus is both God and man (Colossians 2:9; Isaiah 9:6; 2 John 7). Any religion that does not acknowledge Jesus as Lord and Savior is not Christian (1 John 4:1–6).

Significant People

Jesus' disciples—twelve chosen men, including Peter, James, and John, and others.

Paul, who converted to Christianity about five years after Jesus' resurrection and brought Christianity to people throughout the Roman Empire.

Martin Luther (1483–1546), who preached that we are justified by grace alone, through faith in Christ alone, as taught by Scripture alone.

Today's Connection

About one third of the world's population describe themselves as Christian. Though there are many denominations, the Church is united in belief in the triune God, the Bible as God's Word, and salvation through Jesus.

Christian Response

Central to the Christian faith is the belief that Jesus, God's only Son, is both fully human and fully divine. He suffered, died, and rose again so that we might receive God's gift of forgiveness of sins. He fulfilled the Law so that we might receive God's gift of Christ's righteousness.

JUDAISM

History

Traces its roots back to Abraham in 2000 BC. God's promises to Abraham (Genesis 12:1–3) and His covenant with him (Genesis 15:1–21) begin the relationship between God and the Jews.

Central Teaching

God is a personal, all-powerful, eternal, and compassionate God. His history with His people and His basic teachings are found in the *Torah*, the first five books of the Old Testament. Judaism also accepts as true the entire Old Testament and the *Talmud*, a 2,700-page record of the teachings of ancient rabbis.

Significant People

In addition to Abraham, the other Old Testament patriarchs are considered giants of the faith. King David also is revered because under him Israel became a mighty world power.

Today's Connection

There are almost six million Jews living in the United States. Almost every major city has at least one synagogue.

Christian Response

Most Jews will be familiar with Jesus, but they won't acknowledge Him as the Savior. Because of their belief that the Messiah has not yet come, we can witness to Jews by celebrating the hope we have in Jesus. An active, dynamic faith that openly confesses Jesus is the best witness.

Web Resource

www.jewfaq.org/index.htm

ISLAM

History

In AD 610, a businessman named Muhammad (570–632), who lived in Mecca in Saudi Arabia, began to preach submission to the one God, Allah. He claimed that he did this as a result of a vision of the angel Gabriel, who gave him the *Qur'an*, Islam's sacred scriptures. Today, Islam is the religion of about 21 percent of the world's population.

Central Teaching

The central confession in Islam is the *shahada*, "There is no God but Allah, and Muhammad is his prophet." *Muslim* means "one who submits." Islam teaches submission to God in all things. It is a code of honor, a system of law, and a way of life based on the Qur'an. The level of devotion to the moral code determines one's salvation.

Significant People

Muhammad, the founder of Islam, is considered Allah's last and greatest prophet. Muslims also believe that Abraham, Moses, and Jesus are great prophets. Jesus is not considered to be God's Son or the Messiah.

Today's Connection

Islam is the world's fastest-growing religion. Some experts have predicted that the number of Muslims will surpass the number of Christians as early as 2025. Islam is especially active on college campuses and in large communities.

Christian Response

The important Christian teaching to keep in mind when encountering Islam is that Jesus is not just a prophet: He is the Son of God, Savior of the world, and God's promised Messiah, who died on the cross for the forgiveness of our sins.

Web Resource

islamworld.net

Hinduism

History

One of the world's oldest religions, Hinduism developed between 1800 and 1000 BC in India. Hinduism contains many sects. Hinduism is both a religion and a way of life. It is described in the *Vedas* (considered the world's most ancient scriptures, about 1000 BC) and the *Bhagavad-Gita*, an eighteen-chapter poem.

Central Teaching

Hindus believe that all things are part of God, that souls are reincarnated at death, and that our lives are influenced by *karma* (good and bad actions in this life determine one's status in the next). The goal is *moksha*, release from *samsara* or the cycle of reincarnation, to become one with God.

Significant People

Hinduism developed over many centuries; there is no single significant founder or leader. The most famous among its followers is Mahatma Gandhi, who led India to freedom from the British Empire in the early twentieth century.

Today's Connection

The New Age and transcendental meditation are popular movements with roots in Hinduism. Meditation and yoga have become common forms of stress release in our society, with classes offered at local fitness and community centers.

Christian Response

According to God's Word, salvation is found only in the saving work of the triune God (Acts 4:12). Although Christians are to live in obedience to God, their salvation is not dependent on their obedience (Ephesians 2:8–9).

Web Resource

uwacadweb.uwyo.edu/religionet/er/hindu ism/index.htm

BUDDHISM

History

Buddhism arose in India about 500 BC. Siddhartha Gautama found that his Hindu beliefs did not adequately explain the suffering and pain he observed in the world. Through religious contemplation, Gautama became *Buddha*, "the enlightened one," and taught his discoveries.

Central Teaching

Pure Buddhism is more philosophy than religion, a godless pietism. Other forms of Buddhism revere Buddha as a deity and speak of salvation through faith in him. Buddhism is a journey to an enlightened state of being. People do this by accepting the Four Noble Truths and following the Eightfold Path.

Significant People

Founder: Siddhartha Gautama (Buddha) about 563–483 BC. Other major teachers: Nichiren, AD 1222–1282 in Japan, and the Dalai Lama, currently living in exile from Tibet in Dharmasala, India.

Today's Connection

Buddhism has gained popularity among media and sports celebrities worldwide. The *middle road* and balanced life of Buddhism are a welcome change from a celebrity life. Today, followers number over three hundred million worldwide, between two and five million in the United States.

Christian Response

Salvation is not achieved by right thoughts and right things. It is a gift given to us by a personal God through the sacrifice of His Son. We receive this gift by faith.

Web Resource

www.buddhanet.net

SIKHISM

History

Guru Nanak was the first prophetic teacher of Sikhism. After his death, he was succeeded by one guru after another, all of which acted as prophets of Sikhism. At the time of the tenth guru, Gobind Rai (1675–1708), two developments occurred within the new religion. First, it was declared that the line of the gurus had come to an end. Second, the writings and hymns of the previous gurus were collected in a text called the *Siri Guru Granth Sahib*. The *Guru Granth* is the Sikh's primary source of religious authority.

Central Teaching

Sikhism is a compilation of Hindu and Muslim beliefs. It teaches that there is one God, who created all things. But it also teaches that the created souls are forever caught up in the cycle of reincarnation (*samsara*) until they are able to escape it through the discipline of meditation.

Significant People

The founder of Sikhism was a religious teacher named Guru Nanak (1469–1539). He lived in what is now called Pakistan. Sikh tradition recounts how Nanak had a vision that he was to preach and teach a new religion. Shortly thereafter, when he was bathing in a stream, he disappeared and was sent into seclusion, only to return three days later to proclaim the principle teaching of Sikhism. When asked questions, his only response was "There is no Hindu, there is no Muslim."

Today's Connection

Approximately 75 percent of Sikhs live in the Punjab region of India, yet significant populations of Sikhs can be found in major cities worldwide, primarily due to individuals who have migrated from Pakistan and India. Traditional Sikhs keep their hair long, although it is typically kept under a turban.

Christian Response

While rejecting the pantheistic gods of Hinduism for the concept of a single god, Sikhs do not worship the one true God. In addition to sharing the Gospel, it is vital to explain how all have sinned and fallen short of the glory of God, for without the Law, the Gospel is irrelevant.

Web Resource

www.sikhnet.com/pages/introduction-sikhism

SHINTO

History

Shinto, the native religion of Japan, is one of the oldest religions in the world, combining ancient religious practices with such influences as Buddhism and Confucianism.

Central Teaching

Shinto is primarily a form of nature worship. Mountains, rivers, heavenly bodies, and other things are worshiped and personified. Rules, rituals, and worship of kami (spirit) help to maximize agricultural harvests and bring blessings to social units or territories while preventing destruction and ill fortune.

Significant People

Shinto has no real founder, no written scriptures, no body of religious law, and only a very loosely organized priesthood. Shinto is a non-exclusive religion, that is, people may practice Shinto along with a second or even third religion.

Today's Connection

North America has a large population of Japanese immigrants. They continue to practice their Shinto beliefs even as they adapt and "try out" other religions.

Christian Response

We have a powerful message to share with those of the Shinto faith—Jesus Christ has paid everything we owe, performed all the duties that are required, suffered, died, and rose from death so that we can be free from sin and have new life in Him.

Web Resource

www.dlshq.org/religions/shintoism.htm

CONFUCIANISM AND DAOISM

History

Confucianism and Daoism both emerged in ancient China. Around 500 BC, various feudal lords were locked in political and military conflict. This is known as the period of the Warring States. In the aftermath of the turmoil, many people began to ask how China could become reunited. Solutions were proposed by hundreds of intellectuals during the period of the Hundred Schools.

Central Teaching

Confucius claimed that harmony with the *Dao* was best attained by restoring order in society. Confucianism sees the family as the bedrock of society. Therefore, proper relationships at home between children, parents, grandparents, and even deceased ancestors (by veneration) needed to be instituted.

Laozi focused not on society but on nature. Nature, he taught, contained five elements—metal, earth, wood, fire, and water—and was empowered by two energies—yin (male) and yang (female). Harmony with the *Dao* and even immortality could be achieved by balancing the elements and energies.

Significant People

By far the two most influential thinkers were Confucius and Laozi. They both taught (in their respective writings—the *Analects of Confucius* and the *Dao de jing*) that the only way for society to recover from the political and socio-cultural devastation of the Warring States period was for Chinese society to realign itself with the *Dao*, the way or path, in which the universe was moving.

Today's Connection

Today many Chinese embrace the teachings of Confucius as their ethical code of conduct and the mysterious notions of Daoism in their private, meditative life. How many is unclear, but it is surely also to be found throughout the large population of Asian Americans.

Christian Response

Confucianism and Daoism both fall into the trap of worshiping the creation rather than the creator. As Christians, we acknowledge Jesus Christ as Lord and Savior and that only through His death and resurrection can salvation be found.

Web Resource

www.daoism.net

confucianism.freehostingguru.com

MORMONISM

THE CHURCH OF JESUS CHRIST OF LATTER-DAY SAINTS

History

The Church of Jesus Christ of Latter-day Saints was formed by Joseph Smith Jr. in 1830 in Fayette, New York. Smith claims to have translated the Book of Mormon from golden tablets entrusted to him by the angel Moroni. In 1844, Smith and his brother were imprisoned and killed. Brigham Young moved the group to the Salt Lake Valley, where it flourished.

Central Teaching

Mormons believe that God was once a human being just like us and that we can become gods and earn admittance to a celestial heaven.

Significant People

In addition to Joseph Smith (1805–1844) and Brigham Young, other important leaders include Oliver Cowdery, who figured prominently in the founding, and Sidney Rigon, an early convert and theologian in the Latter-day Saints who was passed over for leadership at Smith's death.

Today's Connection

Mormon tabernacles have been erected in all parts of the United States and are planned or under construction for all major continents. Mormon membership has grown to more than thirteen million members worldwide with more than five million in the United States. The sight of two young men in business suits and black name tags riding bicycles and knocking on people's doors is familiar to many. These are among the more than fifty thousand volunteer missionaries who serve the church each year.

Christian Response

Christians bear witness to the one triune God, through whom we have salvation by God's grace alone, not by our efforts. The Bible is God's unchanging truth and our only authority for teaching.

Web Resource

www.mormon.org/mormonorg/eng

JEHOVAH'S WITNESSES

History

Charles T. Russell (1852–1916) founded The Watchtower Bible and Tract Society in Pennsylvania in 1884. The group became officially known as Jehovah's Witnesses in 1931. The Witnesses claim worldwide membership of 6.9 million, with approximately one million members in the United States.

Central Teaching

Jehovah's Witnesses believe that they have been organized to announce the early establishment of God's rule on earth. The Witnesses use the *Watchtower* to interpret the Bible and as the main means for spreading their doctrine. They also have their own version of the Bible called the New World Translation.

Significant People

Charles T. Russell was the founder and author of most of the Studies in the Scriptures that outline the group's teachings. His successor, Joseph Rutherford, moved the organization to Brooklyn, New York, and established the governing body, a small group of men who continue to direct the work and determine the teachings of the Witnesses.

Today's Connection

It seems likely that most everyone will encounter Jehovah's Witnesses at their own doorstep at some time or another. Door-to-door witnessing is the only activity of members on which records are kept and is the most important requirement for their salvation.

Christian Response

Christians share three important truths with the Witnesses: (1) the Bible is the only source for all our knowledge about God and His plan for salvation; (2) salvation is not earned by good works, but is ours by God's grace through faith in Jesus Christ; and (3) Jesus Christ is true God, and all who believe in Him have forgiveness of sins and eternal life.

Web Resource

www.watchtower.org

SCIENTOLOGY

History

Scientology was founded in 1954 by L. Ron Hubbard. The movement began with the popularity of Hubbard's self-help book *Dianetics: The Modern Science of Mental Health.*

Central Teaching

Using the methods of Scientology, people are capable of raising their own spiritual awareness to the point of achieving immortality. Those who reach this level are called *operating thetans* (thay-tns).

Significant People

Scientology is based solely on the many writings of L. Ron Hubbard. Among the members of the Church of Scientology are numerous celebrities, including John Travolta, Tom Cruise, Kirstie Alley, and Lisa Marie Presley.

Today's Connection

L. Ron Hubbard's writings are widely available in bookstores. *Dianetics*, his most famous title, is widely marketed as a self-help book. Scientology benefits from endorsements, donations, and public appearances from its celebrity members.

Christian Response

Thanks be to God that as Christians we do not have to rely on ourselves for salvation! In our Baptism, we are claimed by God, "who saved us and called us to a holy calling, not because of our works, but because of His own purpose and grace" (2 Timothy 1:9).

Web Resource

www.Scientology.org

The New Age

History

The modern New Age movement is a postmodern blend of many old religious concepts. It is a loose network of organizations and individuals who believe that humankind can and must "fix" themselves and the world through enlightened thinking, including beliefs from various Eastern religions, the occult, and distortions of Christianity.

Central Teaching

Most New Age followers advocate personal and social transformation through self-development, cosmic evolution, spiritism, and political action. According to New Age thinking, the reason for social problems and disharmony is our failure to realize our unlimited personal potential.

Significant People

The New Age movement adopts the deities, founders, and prophets of other religions as spiritual role models. Jesus, for example, is one of many "ascended masters"—people who recognized their divine capabilities and used them. Celebrities such as Shirley MacLaine and others have been very active in the New Age movement.

Today's Connection

The New Age influence can be seen in modern self-help movements (TM, yoga, and Zen), secular humanism, popular music styles, and movie and television programming.

Christian Response

We are made in the image of God, but we are not God! God is our loving Father—not a force. God offers eternal life, health, and peace only through faith in Jesus Christ as God and Savior from sin.

SATANISM

History

The term *satanism* is applied to many cults and movements, some of which predate the time of Christ and among which there is little unity. Even today, different satanic organizations vary in beliefs and practices.

Central Teaching

Traditional satanism emphasizes worship of a powerful, personal devil through cultic ritual and black magic. This form has not disappeared. Modern satanists frequently reject worship of Satan but advocate instead that everyone indulge in whatever activity they want, without limit or restraint. This often includes satanic practices.

Significant People

Aleister Crowley (1875–1947) was an early leader of modern satanism in Great Britain.

Anton Szandor LaVey (1930–1997) was the force behind modern satanism. In 1966, LaVey formed the Church of Satan. He wrote *The Satanic Bible* and *The Satanic Rituals*.

Today's Connection

Satanism is a do-it-yourself religion that can spring up anywhere. It is usually stumbled into by unsuspecting people who are open to its lies because they seek excitement, easy solutions to their problems, or power over others through magic.

Christian Response

The truth of God's Word is a powerful weapon against the lies of Satan. Christians can share the truth of Jesus Christ with Satan's followers, confident that he has ultimately been crushed through Christ's suffering, death, and resurrection.

Web Resource

www.modernsatanism.com/satanism.html

RASTAFARIANISM

History

Rastafarianism has its roots in a Black Nationalist movement begun by a Jamaican named Marcus Garvey (1887–1940). In 1927, he announced that in the future a leader would emerge from Africa who would deliver the black urban masses. Three years later, in Ethiopia, Ras Tafari Makonnen (1892–1975) was crowned Emperor Haile Selassie and given the title "King of Kings, Lord of Lords, His Imperial Majesty of the Conquering Lion of the Tribe of Judah, Elect of God." He was seen by many Jamaicans as a great liberator of blacks, but eventually his admirers would identify him in messianic if not divine terms.

Central Teaching

Many Rastafarians believe Selassie is still alive today, and thus they acknowledge him as a supreme being. Rastafarianism (and even more so the Nation of Islam) asserts the superiority of what it calls the black race. Because whites are largely responsible for bringing blacks out of their African homeland to places in the West like Jamaica and the West Indies, Rastafarianism reserves a special hatred for the white race. It envisions a future where blacks will take their vengeance out on whites and return to the homeland of Ethiopia, where God (*Jah*) will rule over them in what will be a heaven on earth.

Significant People

While the crowning of Emperor Haile Selassie in Ethiopia began the Rastafarian movement in Jamaica, it remained little known until reggae music hit the mainstream. The popularity of reggae artist Bob Marley brought the Rastafarian lifestyle and beliefs into the mainstream.

Today's Connection

There are probably about 1 million Rastafarians across the world today. Only about five thousand live in America. Some aspects of Rastafarianism are now making a comeback and have become popularized. This is primarily due the influence of reggae music. Dreadlocks and the consumption of marijuana—both part and parcel of Rastafarianism—are now part of popular culture.

Christian Response

God calls all people as His own. "For as many of you as were baptized into Christ have put on Christ. There is neither Jew nor Greek, there is neither slave nor free, there is no male and female, for you are all one in Christ Jesus" (Galatians 3:27–28).

Web Resource

altreligion .about.com/ library/faqs/bl_ rastafarianism .htm

ATHEISM

History

The roots of atheism can be seen in the sixteenth century, but modern atheism was developed in the nineteenth and twentieth centuries.

Central Teaching

Atheists believe there is no god. They argue that there are no rational or intellectual grounds to believe in God.

Significant People

Notables include Karl Marx (1818–1883), Friedrich Nietzsche (1844–1900), and Jean-Paul Sartre (1905–1981). Madalyn Murray O'Hair (1919–1995) gained prominence in America through her fight to end the practice of daily Bible reading and prayer in public schools and the founding of the organization American Atheism. Ironically, one of her sons later was baptized and became a Baptist minister.

Today's Connection

Atheism tends to be a less aggressive and organized movement. Many of their advocates create campus organizations and advertise through Internet Web sites.

Christian Response

The atheists of this world miss an important truth: our certainty about God and the salvation He has provided for us in His Son comes through faith, which is God's gracious gift as the Holy Spirit works through the Word.

Web Resource

www.atheist.org/Atheism